Keeley's Kures

Alternative practices from the trails and trials of a world-champion hobo-adventurer

By Bo Keel

Free Man Publishing Co.

Published 2011 by Free Man Publishing Co.

Keeley's Kures:
Alternative practices from the trails and trials of a world-champion hobo-adventurer

Available via Amazon.com and other bookstores. For larger quantity orders and other inquiries: inquiries@keeleykures.com

Printed in the United States of America

Disclaimer

The author and publisher of *Keeley's Kures* are not physicians; we doubt any of the statements in this book has been evaluated by the FDA or any other coercive-government entity. No statement in this book should be construed as curative advice or recommendation except as it exercises First Amendment-acknowledged freedom of judgment or opinion of the author applying to his own conditions—real or potential. The author and publisher are not trying to persuade you to adopt any particular health-care practice. We do encourage readers to use all available resources to form their own opinions and judgments about how to take care of themselves.

Dedication

To Doc Brooks in Blythe, California:

Ex-prize fighter, piano player for the Grateful Dead, Cesar Chavez's personal physician in the fields, and who treated me gratis after I bled through a hundred shirts from a backpack wound that a dozen physicians and hospitals across America wouldn't or didn't know how to handle.

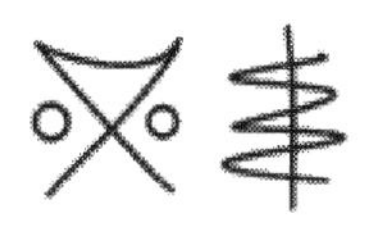

Physicians and politicians resemble one another in this respect, that some defend the constitution and others destroy it.
— Author Unknown

FOREWORD

Whence comes the good fortune to encounter so unique a person as Bo Keeley—credentialed in medicine (DVM), former national racquet-sport champion, blue-collar budget traveler, adventurer, peak natural-experience chaser… and common ailment researcher? Then to be asked to do his book?

Thankfully, yours truly was in the right place at the right time: Bo was e-introduced to me through a Michigan liberty icon, Dean Hazel, as another rare individual who prefers to 'color outside the lines.' And outside the country much of the time.

First impressions: With a tentative grasp, I quickly discovered several excellent writings from 'Doc' Keeley, many posted on *dailyspeculations.com* and *swanscommentary.com*. Then following some engaging and entertaining e-back-and-forth, Bo gave me permission to use some of his material in Guest Columns on my own site, *thecoffeecoaster.com*.

Second impressions: Dr. Keeley has the literary snap of late Gonzo journalist Hunter S. Thompson… w/o the drugs or reckless discharge of firearms.

Third impressions: When it comes to practical responses to what ails real people, Bo *knows* stuff, and conveys it with uncommon sensitivity and wit. You'll surely enjoy this journey and those to come.

Brian Wright, Editor and Proprietor
Free Man Publishing Co.

Contents

INTRODUCTION

This publication grew out of frustration with conventional medicine and a health system that dissuades natural, home treatments. The information sources, then, are not so awkward.

I took a doctorate degree in veterinary medicine on the road to 100+ countries observing medical treatments in hospitals, psych wards, and prisons. Boxcar medicine from the American railroads provided seat-of-the-pants therapies when no doctor was around. As well, hiking the lengths of Colorado, Florida, Vermont, California, and Baja contributed to wilderness medicine.

The Kures—practices I believe most will see as cures with a "c"—are used on myself, or informally on acquaintances. They are original, usually successful, and arise outside conventional medicine in veterinary clinics, American boxcars, and around the world in resolving assorted common ailments.

A cheerful frame of mind, reinforced by options of alternative medicine, may mend, and put the ghosts of fear of traditional doctors and hospitals on the run. The author and publisher are not physicians, take no responsibility for Kure outcomes, and disclaim that any medical treatment should not be supervised by a doctor.

Steven 'Bo' Keeley, April 2011
Lake Toba, Sumatra

What is it?

The term brings drugs or alcohol to mind, but people also can be addicted to other substances and activities. The striking characteristic is the person may be compelled to something without acquiring gain or pleasure. Other tip-offs are continual use, solitary use, guilt, intimations that one is hooked, slacking at worthier endeavors, inability to hold a job, or financial problems that lead to illegal activities to afford the habit. In the extreme, a person continues without self-regulation until there is nothing left.

Traditional Treatment

Varied, controversial and with ranging degree of cure. The two prongs of addiction—psychological and physiological—are divided and attacked. Possibilities include decreasing doses of substance or activity, quick withdrawal, symptomatic treatment, application of lesser addictive drugs, individual and group support.

Kure

Recovered peer. Repeat that, for it's the key Kure on the path away from addiction. One believes another who precedes him. This observation is from investigating circles of speculators, athletes, hobos, and citizens around the world. Animals also become physiologically and psychologically addicted.

I believe a weak personality becomes addicted to the carrot—something feels good and there is small will to resist again and again. On the other hand, a strong person likely gets addicted from the whip in an attempt to escape the discomforts or difficulties of life. Finding someone who is immune to addiction is unlikely; they simply haven't met their match. This is why parental control of the young and, later, self-control by the mature is imperative. My wrestling coach used to say, "There never was a horse that couldn't be rode nor a man who couldn't be throw'd." The unsusceptible individual is a rare bird.

This entry focuses on general addiction. (Specific comments on individual substances or activities may be found throughout the Kures.) The principles are usually applicable to any addiction. I have been treating a chocolate addict by his own definition. He was Kured with one email summarized as follows:

> "Find a recovered peer. If no one else will do, use me because I used to "do" chocolate as nightly reward to get through college. Remove the substance from sight and have no access to it. Substitute something for the addiction and reach for it instead, such as a piece of bread. For any addictive urge, drink a glass of water before giving in. Find a friend to call or email if you backslide. Next, decide either to kick the habit at once or in degrees. You have the will to do it instantly, but can choose the slower course.

Recovered peer. Repeat that, for it's the key Kure on the path away from addiction.

> "The first method requires deep commitment, whereas gradual withdrawal is decreasing the addictive dose over time. Touch base often

with the recovered peer who is the model of your future self. Stay away from an environment that offers the thing or activity you want to avoid—say, chocolate—for at least six months after kicking the habit. Exercise and drink lots of fluids to vitalize circulation. Note that a workout program also promotes general health, distracts from urges, and encourages discipline. Establish a continual reward system but don't abuse it. Consider a support group. Finally, what is your priority in life? If it's health, then take care of your addiction(s) *now*."

What is it?

Also called mountain sickness, this is an interesting array of symptoms due to a decline of oxygen at increased altitudes. At 8,000 ft., for example, I've learned that about half as much oxygen exists as at sea level. My belief is that lower barometric pressure at high elevation makes inspiration more laborious, so oxygen intake decreases and the symptoms come on. Weekend mountain climbers and pilots rather than high altitude residents get the sickness, and if one ascends gradually to great heights over a week's time he should not suffer.

Traditional Treatment

Oxygen and descent to lower altitude. Mountain climbers use a mixture of air and pure oxygen for treatment, whereas pilots pressurize cabins. Fluids, rest, and symptomatic treatment, which means to treat each symptom as it arises.

Kure

First, encouragement. Don't let high talk keep you out of the mountains. I could reel off personal stories from the Ruwenzoris in Uganda to the Andes in Bolivia, but in each the lesson is that the human body adapts. Experts point to favorable increases in blood volume and red blood cell count during a week or more of acclimation at target elevation, and I underscore this by postulating that each body cell adapts. So acclimate and hike and climb in comfort.

Next: **Insight**. You're on the streets of heaven, alone at 13,000' on some far-flung range. If you've acclimated, fine. But if not apply the lessons from this altitude sickness scale (I've experienced all):

1. You have difficulty sucking air; breathing and pulse are rapid. Don't worry about stage 1.
2. A tinge of headache occurs, that is not serious except if one ignores it as the signpost of step 3, in which **Insight** will be lost.
3. Strange things happen. As with scuba "nitrogen narcosis," one may be disallowed from understanding he is confused. You can stare with a silly grin at a cloud and walk off a cliff to die with a fixed grin. Pain exists but one witnesses it as if from a distance.
4. Reality and body sensation return, and it feels horrible. There may be a pounding head and heart, dizziness, lassitude, and dangerous stumbling. I can walk at this stage for only 100 yards between 5-minute rests.
5. One is on the ground in the mountains and won't recover there. You must descend *now*.

The final tip is the role of water. I drink nearly as much at high elevation as during desert walks probably because of evaporation in the dry atmosphere. The resulting low blood volume produces a 'shock'-like feeling, which is prevented and reversed by liquid replenishment. It's customary for hikers and climbers to reach stage two on the scale routinely, then proceed slowly, aware that if the condition worsens they must find a lower level.

What is it?

When you run from a bear or see a naked spouse, this is good anxiety. When you wake up, walk through the day, and go to bed anxiously, your psyche needs pruning. The feeling may creep up slowly and be upon one practically unaware, or jump aboard as a full panic attack. My belief is that on a base level, anxiety is flight or fright. What isn't?

Symptoms include heightened alertness, worry, perhaps impaired concentration, restlessness, and irritability that can proceed to insomnia, sweating, muscle tightness or trembling, rapid and shallow breathing, excessive fatigue, and maybe hot flashes. Panic attack is so-named for the acute condition. (Acute means sudden and extreme.) There may be a perceived dread, personal showdown with terror, and even fear of dying soon. Some place the causes as endless, from stress to drugs. To talk about anxiety opens a can of worms that makes fishing doctors and shrinks wealthy. The symptoms are real, but intertwine with life itself.

Traditional Treatment

The usual claim is this mysterious condition of myriad causes with unpredictable onset has uncertain treatment. The single factor properly addressed by traditional medicine is prevention; if a cause can be identified, nip it in the bud. Psychotherapy is often suggested, but not by me... before trying the following Kures. The exception is if there is a danger to self or to others. Drugs are the next downhill conventional step. In sum, there is little good about the traditional treatments.

Kure

No problem. Checker player Tom Wiswell once scratched his head in mid-game, "It's too confusing for me. Time to simplify." He cleared the board by trading down pieces. Lest anyone undervalue the advice of this acquaintance, Wiswell won the world checker championship some two dozen times, often in a state of good anxiety. I write adventure articles for magazines and many are excerpts from an ongoing autobiography of perils in deserts, jungles, and mountains. My stability is that when it comes to medicine, the physical underlies the mental almost every time. That is, given a mental condition, it is well to look first for a physical cause. If you accept this premise, the Kures are easy.

Begin by getting fit. Anyone who sees a shrink without exercising daily *needs* his head examined. Also get trim. Humor has value. Drink lots of good liquids (Ref. "Bladder Stones" on page 12) since anxiety has a neurochemical aspect and the idea is to flush the body systems as a spring flood cleans a canyon. Sleep well and warm.

The first thing you do in the morning and last thing at night should be enjoyable. Surround yourself with strong, optimistic people. Recovered peers are invaluable resources. Consider a support group, or a single close friend to help you hurdle the tough moments. Support can be via email too, as the case of a Chicago friend who wrote that panic attacks were ruining his life. I emailed him once a week for a month and he was free to respond as the condition toned down.

Medications are too often crutches, not cures. Use them briefly in a pinch, and then toss them aside. Some anti-anxiety pills would give *anyone* a panic attack, so I'll take a glass of water and a walk any day. Don't smoke or take caffeine. Watch educational TV rather than the news and cop shows, or read a biography about an achiever.

My conviction is that city noise figures in anxiety and panic. Consider moving from the source of irritation. Meditation is excellent. It may be soothing to admit you're nervous and rehearse improvement by mentally picturing your ideal self and gaining on it slowly. Finally, while working as a psych technician I used to tell patients, "At times and places it's normal to be anxious," and they were momentarily stunned, walking away apparently calmed by the reality.

The most outstanding Kure for many psychological conditions including anxiety and panic is to step back and examine priorities. When I was a young man someone once asked me to prioritize the most important things in life. I began with health. "Wait," interrupted the inquirer, "most people list family, job, and financial security." I replied, "What good are you to family, job, or account if you're in a shambles." Put health at the top of life's goals.

What is it?

Breathed air passes the mouth or nose, down the trachea and into small passageways called bronchi within the lungs. Envision what happens if the thin linings of these passageways inflame and swell. There may be sudden breathing difficulty, wheezing, plus rapid-and-shallow breathing, which feels like suffocation. In some people this bronchial asthma rears its ugly head periodically for who knows precisely why.

Traditional Treatment

The normal procedure is to look for a needle in a haystack of alleged irritants. These so-called allergens in the home, work, or hobby environment can include (to name a common few): dust, cold air, nuts, fish, chocolate, and viruses. An asthma treatment ironically may trigger asthma, such as spraying a carpet for dust or mites only to react to the spray. Hence, the condition within conventional medicine is a Pandora's box within a Pandora's box. Most of the present traditional treatments are unsatisfactory; you may be asked to haul around an inhaler or peak flow meter, to pop corticosteroid pills and to endure desensitizing injections.

Kure

I hiked the Colorado Trail, which courses along the Continental Divide from Denver to Durango. One morning, at 14,000 ft., I spotted an elfin figure in black tights cresting a peak and coming toward me. He stopped to talk: "I'm happy and sad at the same time. Today is my last on the trail." He had taken an odd route out of necessity causing him to end the 500-mile hike nearly where I stood. "The experts told me not to attempt this path. I was beginning to feel handicapped by what they said. But look at this." He showed me a large, zip-locked baggy of medicine. "I'm terribly asthmatic, but haven't opened the bag. What's more, I've done something few people can do." The man encouraged me to complete the trail, saying, "The scenes ahead are just like the pictures in the guidebook—nothing doctored."

The embarrassingly broad label of asthma reminds one of the story of the carpenter whose only tool is a hammer so he sees every problem as a nail.

I think many diseases of unknown cause and cure can be treated successfully by emulating the recovery course of a recovered peer. That's where hope and incentive begin. This usually involves exercise. In addition, breathe warm air at night. Wrap the throat with a sweater or towel (ref. "Common Cold," page 19) to insulate the trachea so that the air reaching the bronchi is of a healing temperature. Desert or mountain air is clean air, so if your condition is serious consider a move.

Many professionals miss a nuance about weather in treating respiratory problems in that as the bronchial tubes heal, the best climate for the condition may change. Cold air is fine for the initial inflammation and, in fact, you can stick your face in a freezer for an acute attack. However, chronic mild asthma should respond better to dry warmth if given time.

If you smoke, it's an embarrassment. My nearest desert neighbor at a mile down the road is a two-fisted breather, with an asthma inhaler in one hand and pack of cigarettes in the other. Avoid this.

Drink lots of water, especially if lung mucus is a problem. Bring your blood pressure down. If the asthma is diagnosed as psychological (ref. "Anxiety States and Panic Attacks," page 6), try the physical Kures before pills and shots. Learn to control the relaxation response. Many asthmatic patients are overweight; it is difficult to miss the correlation. Shed excess weight (ref. "Obesity," page 62).

The embarrassingly broad label of asthma reminds one of the story of the carpenter whose only tool is a hammer, so he sees every problem as a nail. It isn't much of a claim, but for a malady that is misdiagnosed 80% of the time, I estimate a 90% Kure rate.

BLADDER STONES

What is it?

When a white substance such as calcium oxalate in the urine concentrates and forms tiny marbles that lodge in the bladder or kidney, you'll know stones. Normally these calculuses are teensy enough that they are carried like flotsam in a small river and excreted. But if a stone lodges in, say, the neck of the bladder, then more substance can layer on over time and it enlarges with sharp faces. The symptoms are pain, urinary blockage, or infection. Just as rough, over history, has been identifying the cause of stones.

Traditional Treatment

The convention of limiting a diet of high oxalic acid is sensible. Spinach, leafy vegetables, and coffee are to be avoided by this rule. Drink lots of liquids. There are analgesics (painkillers) for comfort. Smaller stones can be removed using a cystoscope, a tube for viewing and removing, while larger ones can be extracted surgically. Other possibilities are sound or shock waves to render the stones smaller for natural removal during urination.

Kure

Drink distilled water. My former banker in northern California was a chipper middle-aged lady who had degenerated into a sad affair over a period of a month. She started coming to work with a grimaced face, red-eyed from crying and pasty-skinned from medication. Since it was a small town with a one-person branch operation, she couldn't miss work. She broke down one day and told me that the pain of bladder stones and failed treatments had ruined her life.

I asked when the symptoms had begun and she responded that they started in a small way three years prior, a year after moving to the community. Were there others in the area with the same diagnosis, I asked. She said yes, and named some neighbors. She and the others were on medications to dissolve the stones, sonic shocks to shatter them, and pain killers to make life bearable. Some were facing surgery.

The Kure was simply to let the body flush out the stones—by drinking tremendous quantities of distilled water—and at the same time not add to them. "I've been drinking lots of water per doctor's orders," she lamented. But it was tap water which was adding layers to the stones. She switched and began carrying a jug of distilled water everywhere, even making distilled ice Kubes. Coffee she hadn't given up, which is understandably hard in such a time of toil, so I told her the secret to getting off coffee or tea is to drink a full glass of warm water before allowing the coffee. She found, as do the majority, that following heated water there is little taste for coffee or tea.

In a week the bloom was back in her cheeks and she was off medicines including the painkillers. In a month, she was symptom free. She spread the word to others in the area and was considering starting a Website for the treatment.

Think of yourself as a water transport system—it goes into the mouth and out in the urine—in order to grasp the importance of water and water type in your life. A short course on water may be a vital medical lesson. I divide drinkable water into four types: distilled, bottled spring, bottled drinking, and tap water. Distilled water is essentially the same as rainwater from the sky. It is commonly sold in supermarkets for use in irons and car batteries because it's pure and mineral-free. Minerals can be said to contribute to clogging the iron, blood vessels, and urinary tract via stones.

Distilled water is my preferred drink. The next best type is bottled spring water from the same market. Spring water is untainted unlike almost all city-treated water and bottled drinking water. As the name implies, it is taken from an underground spring. The little desert town where I live nonetheless boasts two spring water companies that deliver 100-gallon containers in an oceanic business. Spring water has dissolved minerals and is fine except for the calculus or arteriosclerotic patient. Bottled drinking water, on the other hand, is only sometimes good and often no better than tap water because most is processed with toxic substances just like city water. Tap water is touted by some cities but is anti-Kure to health. In my town the nursery won't use it on plants.

Distilled water is my preferred drink. The next best type is bottled spring water.

The message here is water increases fluid output from the body and, along with it, the stones. If the water is distilled no minerals exist to build stones. Augment this with the dietary treatment, and consider one of the teas from a green pharmacy designed to dissolve stones. These, and recipes, may be obtained from a health food store or a holistically oriented doctor. The term green pharmacy refers to natural remedies such as herbs, while holistic means taking a wide view in the diagnosis and treatment of a condition. Also, as implied often in this book, holistic means recognizing that leaves and branches (symptoms) of a disease are attached to its roots (true causes), for which there are Kures.

Carpal Tunnel Syndrome

What is it?

This is when the hand and wrist (of one or both arms) becomes numb, tingly, or painful from overuse, especially following long periods of such activities as typing, tennis, knitting, or canoeing. The computer keyboard has brought the condition to public light, and now hundreds of thousands complain of it. It occurs when the median nerve, which courses through a narrow tunnel of wrist bones and by a ligament at the base of the hand, is pressed on by surrounding tissues. The nerve becomes painfully inflamed.

Traditional Treatment

A wrist pad at the base of keyboards, and wrist splints. Some take medication for pain and inflammation. People quit jobs and collect compensation.

Kure

One cue from having spent a lifetime in sports is that a musculoskeletal injury should be handled before it gets serious enough to see the doctor. Similar examples are shin splints to the runner, tennis elbow to a racquet player, and "sore all over" to the school athlete after the first day of practice. Technically, musculoskeletal refers to muscle and skeleton, but I include carpal tunnel syndrome in the category, too. Envision a nerve as a string that courses through tissues and bones. If overused, it and the tissues surrounding it will swell and hurt in response.

Unique Kures exist, the first of which is preventive. The athlete learns that if his body parts are fit then he probably won't get sore shins, elbows, or "all over." Similarly, in anticipation of a new secretarial job that involves computer work, the first thing to do is get the wrist and hands in shape. I came up with a technique for this that enabled me to win several national paddle and racquet championships, where a strong hand rules. Think of the hand not as a unit but a system of levers and pulleys. Exercise each finger independently. Moreover, work the weakest link of the system—the smallest finger—the most because a chain is as strong as its weakest link.

Make up your own exercises, but most will be a simple matter of pressing the fingers one at a time against a stationary object such as a tabletop, wall, hand squeezer, or rubber ball. Important but forgotten by even professional trainers is that a set of muscles usually has an opposing set. So, exercise the tops (extensors) as well as the palmer (flexors) sides of the fingers. Don't forget the sides. I promise dramatic results for sports performance and prevention of hand and wrist injury such as carpal syndrome.

I have an invention that I think will circumvent carpal syndrome as well as revolutionize the modern keyboard and typewriter. The keys will be thimbles rather than one-surface keys. Each thimble will strike in four directions—four characters—up, down, left, and right. Typing speed will be increased by about 25 percent and there will be stronger fingers everywhere because they will press in all, rather than just one, directions.

If you already have carpal syndrome, you have three choices. Work through the pain at the risk of permanent injury, take frequent breaks at the risk of a boss's frown, or take time off to rest and practice the Kures. A few years back, I sat at a computer 8 hours a day for 365 days straight, and had only the slightest hint of any wrist problem. This was accomplished by varying the height of the keyboard by layering books or boards under it every hour or so. I also placed a board in front of the keyboard for the heels of the hands to rest on, and periodically changed its height.

One of the odder and more workable Kures was wearing mittens or gloves to bed. Sleep is the most underestimated healer in life, and the most overlooked aspect of healing is warmth. (ref. "Cuts and Scrapes," page 27). So, for prevention or treatment of carpal syndrome, wear something loose on your hand as you sleep. Additionally, sleep on your back so the hands lay with palms up, which extends and relaxes the tendons that have been pulling in a direction that causes the syndrome. With such innovations, carpal syndrome should be all but medically erased in the future.

What is it?

It's a general term, as well as a condition, for a group of minor, contagious viral infections of the respiratory tract. It is characterized by inflammation of the mucous lining of the nose and throat with the resulting garden variety of symptoms such as sore throat and coughing.

Traditional Treatment

The usual fare is warm rest, aspirin, plenty of fluids, gargles, and possibly antibiotics.

Kure

The most common call I get goes like this: "My god, my throat's killing me and I cough so much I've had to go into cloister. Any advice?" I concur with conventional therapy, but it falls short. If your doctor says drink lots of fluids, I remark double that and make sure that if it's water it's distilled or spring (ref. "Bladder Stones," page 12). The gargle of your choice should be warmed. I think aspirin is a wonder drug, yet I gave it up long ago in favor of weathering out conditions. This is an individual choice. Use antibiotics only as a last resort. Any pill you take should be with a glass of warm water before, with the medication, and a third after. Now here is the meat of what I've learned from years as a disease guinea pig:

Remember the value of warmth in healing. As my ninth grade science teacher pointed out, heating causes expansion. Drink warm fluids. I'm an old-fashion believer in hot chicken soup, though avoid chicken when healthy. The more you drink the more you increase your blood volume, and this increase in blood flow brings in an army of white blood cell soldiers and flushes out the battle wastes. If you're accustomed to exercise, continue unless the cold is particularly severe. I stopped getting colds a decade ago, but prior to this there was not one that I didn't run or play through to the added benefit of the ongoing treatment. Concurrently, I made sure to get an extra hour of sleep each night while sick.

The most significant contribution I have for cold treatment is the throat wrap during sleep. In northern climes, in which I was raised, wintertime meant wrapping the house water pipes to prevent freezing. Most people I've advised find that insulating their body pipes also works wonders. Think about it: each breath of air multiplied by hundreds over the night is warmed and that warmth is transferred to the inflamed mucous linings of the nose, throat, and lungs. Knot the wrap at the back of the neck so it doesn't come loose. Get rid of the pillow to aid drainage and sleep on your back to give the heart pump a rest. Wear gloves and booties if cold phalanges awaken you.

A life of worry about whose hand you shake, glass you share, and lips you touch is a mockery: as unnecessary as the alcohol swab the doctor rubs on the skin before giving an injection for, say a common cold. The point is microbes are everywhere, remindful of Holy Spirit sermons, without and within. Some are good guys and some cause disease. Be clean but not antiseptic. Personally, I grew up welcoming a new disease in order to observe its progress and my reaction; I had to chase kids to catch something. My first cold was like going to the rodeo. Understandably, not everyone wants to play guinea pig but neither should they develop a germ phobia.

A moment to define terms: Inflammation means redness, swelling, warmth, and pain. Inflammation is the body's natural attempt to combat the invading virus that supposedly causes the common cold. Often a patient combats the symptom of inflammation and unwittingly undermines the body's defense against the infection. Infection means there is a presence of a microbe, such as a virus or bacteria.

I have a sense that Vitamin C mega-dose is helpful but don't endorse it as a Kure. As for medications, I worship their capacities, fear their consequences, and avoid taking them when possible. I've been knocked down by dozens of diseases around the globe but the only one that really kept me down was a common cold in veterinary school that developed into a secondary bronchial infection. There were extenuating circumstances in those days that predated Kures:

After two months of hacking I came up with a three-punch combination. The first was a choice from the many over-the-counter cough suppressants which contain Dextromethorphan, a drug that turns off the brain's cough center. The second was oral antibiotics sneaked from the animal medicine chest. And the third was movement to keep the body systems good to go. The result was rosy health in a week, and the edge of this anecdote is if there is a secondary infection with the common cold, see a doctor. He'll explain that a secondary infection is the result of a body weakened by the primary attack, and know what to do.

As for medications, I worship their capacities, fear their consequences, and avoid taking them when possible.

In sum: do nothing and your cold will last seven days, do everything and it will last a week… or take the Kures and it will be halved.

Cardiopulmonary Resuscitation (CPR)

What is it?

Cardiopulmonary resuscitation (CPR) is a combination of chest compressions and rescue breathing delivered to victims thought to be in cardiac arrest, or with stopped breathing. CPR alone is unlikely to restart the heart, and it's main purpose is to restore partial flow of oxygenated blood to the heart and brain in the 'Golden Minute' after cardiac arrest or an accident to buy time until normal heart function is restored.

Traditional Treatment

The trend of first-aid from the old Boy Scout and American Red Cross methods of tourniquets, cutting and sucking a snake bite, and CPR has followed a sad parallel evolution of self-reliance and analysis to relying on others and covering your buttocks.

Kure

The bottom line is would you want an old Boy Scout, or a wannabe thinker, over you in the Golden Minute of an emergency? What you decide to do often hinges on the customs and laws of the country you are in. Consider one of my adventures in Vietnam.

Let Him Die or Risk Life Imprisonment?

The National Road A1, vetted as a bicycle route for Westerners, threads 1000 km of jungles, rice paddies and mountains from Hanoi to Saigon. It's a race from start to finish connecting the metropolises at either end of Vietnam, with much of the traffic collective taxis, minivans, and lumbering buses chasing awaiting passengers. Every driver has a Buddha statue on the dash that he places next to gifts of incense, bread, and alcohol for protection, and they nod to each other during close calls.

The first day out of Hanoi, after a high-speed chase on the back of a motorcycle down alleys and sidewalks, waving increasing increments of Dong (currency) before the driver's helmet, I caught a southbound minivan. Then there were two foreshadows: an oil pan dashed chicken and a taxi fender bender.

The drivers make accelerating pit stops at roadside cafes for coffee and lusty hits off a three-foot tobacco bong—strong stuff that threw me for a loop after a scientific whiff. Then it's back to road fever.

The second day brought the acid test of my Hippocratic Oath as a veterinarian and good hobo Samaritan. Our driver braked hard at 80 km/hr., and the woman in the front seat screamed. Through the windshield a youth, next to his decumbent motorbike, wearing one shoe, lay in the shattered headlamp of a hit-and-run car on the center stripe.

It was fresh with a dozen-member circle of Innocent Bystanders, as I stepped inside to inspect…

My EMT instructor always said, "There's a 'Golden Minute' to treat an accident victim. Some day you will be in it."

The youth lies in a fetal position on a pool of blood, unmoving, no detectable respiration, and a pallor cloaked by natural copper skin. No one in the circle of thirty moves.

I step toward the body, hesitate, and scan my peers' faces.

An Innocent Bystander is a watcher, onlooker, a guiltless witness of a crime or accident. Pounds of bloody psychology dissect every imaginable angle... except today's. If this were the South, or a freer state, rather than the holdover iron-fist communist North, I would step up.

My EMT instructor always said, "There's a 'Golden Minute' to treat an accident victim. Someday you will be in it."

Should I let him die, or risk life imprisonment?

I fall back on veterinary and boxcar medicine in emergencies: Artificial respiration placing my mouth over a kitten's face, pounding an old Boxer's heart with a hand heel, plenty of belts and brassieres in the gathering crowd for tourniquets, my Converse Chucks and shoestrings as a neck splint, and bubblegum plugs a pneumothorax hole-in-the-chest.

In the U.S.A. the unwritten Good Samaritan law protects bystanders who aid a victim from molestation, but in North Vietnam it's the opposite, especially for a Westerner. Conniving kin summon police-on-the-take to the Samaritan for arrest and detention until a deal is cut.

I have a choice.

The second I step out the Golden Minute into the thickening ring, vehicles trumpet. I snap a photo...

And live with it.

Traffic lines the road as far as the eye can see in either direction for an hour, until a gallant Vietnamese bucks political correctness and scoops up the body, slings it over his motorcycle, withers like a wounded cowboy, and bolts down the center stripe.

CUTS AND SCRAPES

What is it?

A cut is a little slice into the skin, and a scrape is a more horizontal rough removal of a patch of skin. There can be blood and some pain but both wounds described here are minor enough to be self-treated.

Traditional Treatment

Stop the bleeding, wash it, keep it clean, smear on antibacterial ointment, bandage it and wait. Possibly check your tetanus shot currency.

Kure

Let it bleed clean. Stop the bleeding after a minute with cold running water or ice. (This cut isn't serious enough for a pressure point.) Keep it out of dirt. Don't put anything on it or bandage it, and keep it from drying out. Next day begin moving the wounded area with exercise, especially if it's near a joint or at the end of extremity. Over ensuing days, keep the scab from being knocked more than once; if this does happen a second time, then bandage it. All coverings should be removed at night.

My methods may not be readily accepted by a microbe over-reactive society, but they're my custom. I began experimenting on myself with various cut and scrape treatments after watching pets, wild animals, mechanics, and street people recover from wounds with little concern and less cleanliness. It was appalling in the face of the germ theory I learned in school. Now I accept that for a healthy individual a cut or scrape heals great 90 percent of the time without a glance. The cut bleeds clean, clots by itself, gets cleaned in the course of the next bath, scabs and heals perfectly. A pet or mechanic may lick it now and then.

> *Now I accept that for a healthy individual a cut or scrape heals great 90 percent of the time without a glance.*

The gradual benefit of not treating is the immune system builds over the years so one may endure greater wounds with faster healing. The 10 percent of the wounds that get mild infection cannot be forgotten, and are treated unceremoniously by the aforementioned groups by draining the pus and squirting on alcohol. I can't recommend that the general population allow wounds to heal without attention beyond water cleansing, but it's tempting; that's what I do because there's too much to do in life to linger on the nicks.

Some cuts require an over-the-counter topical antibiotic. If a wound won't close, if the scab keeps coming loose, if protracted infection occurs or lymph nodes become involved, if insects abound in the area, or you're in a jungle, apply an ointment. Cover the cut only if a lot of dirt or insects are present. I have a superior method of applying topical antibiotic or any surface cream for that matter. I discovered it one winter night in my desert trailer after I had burned my thigh on a Mr. Heater (a portable propane heater that has a round, 8-in.

heating element that gets hot to the touch, as I discovered).

Serendipity struck. On a whim, I applied ointment to a festering cut I had elsewhere and placed it close to Mr. Heater's face. The heat caused the ointment to melt into the skin and be absorbed; it was excitingly like an intradermal (within the skin) injection. Since that night I've also used a match, candle, and incandescent light to facilitate the rapid absorption of topical medications.

Lacking heat, do you suppose there are reasons animals instinctively lick their wounds? There is cleansing, comfort, and I suspect the main reason is to increase circulation to the spot. I recall an early lesson in veterinary surgery as I scrubbed Betadine antiseptic onto the pre-surgical site of a dachshund abdomen. A resident instructor approached as the dog lay awaiting the scalpel under anesthesia and chided me, "Rubbing a surgical site greatly increases the circulation under the skin. Just watch how he bleeds when the incision is made." And it did.

The lesson here is that the goal of healing is to bring blood with its antibodies to the site. I recommend rubbing in an ointment for at least a full minute. This melts the ointment just like Mr. Heater, takes the antibiotic deeper into the tissue where microorganisms reside, and brings circulation to the skin. The rub need not be vigorous, just long in duration.

On the rare occasion a bandage is required, here's a tip from a recent desert hike. There was a dime-sized, weeping sore on my back directly under where the backpack presses the scapula (shoulder blade). A Band-Aid wouldn't stick under the friction and summer sun, so I put a wide strip of duct tape on the dried area. It adhered for hours. And duct tape comes in skin colors! ☺

The lesson here is that the goal of healing is to bring blood with its antibodies to the site.

In sum, for a cut:

- ☐ Let it bleed a bit.
- ☐ Use a topical antiseptic only on deep or dirty wounds. (Preheat the antiseptic to skin temperature to aid absorption.)
- ☐ Keep it uncovered and reasonably clean. (If it requires a Band-Aid for dirty work, try duct tape over a tiny square of paper towel.)
- ☐ The day after receiving a cut, exercise the wound with movement to increase circulation.

What is it?

Freezing of skin with possible damage to underlying blood vessels and tissues. The ears, nose, fingers, and toes are most susceptible (ref. "Hypothermia," page 47).

Traditional Treatment

Warmth.

Kure

My upbringing as an active outdoor kid in northern Michigan and Idaho gave rise to ideas for hypothermia (ref. "Hypothermia," page 49) and frostbite. In Idaho I learned two medical facts from ice-skating. Pressure on the skin plus cold gives a more penetrating freeze than cold only. Sadly, frostbite can increase the likelihood of the same spot suffering in the future. Happily, at the same time I learned to combat the condition by layering socks inside oversized boots and skates not only for warmth but also against the pressure of shoelaces.

In Michigan, I learned from freezing my fingers often that mittens are better than gloves because the fingers heat each other in proximity. For treatment I used a three-pronged Kure:

- ☐ Place the hands in warm water
- ☐ Drink warm fluids
- ☐ Move the fingers

Thus, the heat in treatment should come from without, within, and intrinsically via movement. Later, in hoboing freights on the winter "High Line" route from Minneapolis to Spokane, I discovered the additive effect of wind chill to cold in bringing on frostbite and avoided it by selecting inside "rides" such as boxcars.

Finally, as a cold weather bicycler and distance runner around the world in which I had several bouts with penis frostbite, the remedy was found to wear a sock. I never brought it up to anyone else out of embarrassment until after reading in a *New England Journal of Medicine* that many outdoorsmen had the same problem and the publication recommended the sock, too.

What is it?

A miserable feeling after drinking too much alcohol at one time. Tolerance varies, but everyone reaches his limit.

Traditional Treatment

Head in hand, it's commonly thought no cure exists for a hangover. Drink lots of water, take pain relievers and apply a cold pack for the headache, then nap it off. Tomato juice, and vitamin C to increase the rate of breakdown in the body, plus a dozen such entries as ginger and wintergreen from your green pharmacy or raw eggs from Pliny the Roman elder. Thankfully, the symptoms last only 24 hours, but we can do better than that.

Kure

I don't bring much experience to the drinking table, but as a keen observer in spending nearly 3500 straight one-hour nightly non-drinking sessions, learning body language in bars across America and around the globe, I offer strong second-hand Kures.

Admittedly, I've had two bouts over the decades with alcohol. The first was as a college freshman to answer a claim that one may acquire a taste for beer. I drank two beers a night for a month and personally proved the theory wrong. Years later, I hopped out a boxcar in Wilmington, Delaware, to amble into a skid row bar thirsty and thinking I hadn't given alcohol a chance. An inveterate quantifier, despite being under the influence, I spaced 12 shots of whiskey every 15 minutes, and three hours later staggered into the weeds. The next morning I was not covered with mosquito bites, the bugs were probably inebriated, or at least I didn't feel them for the hangover. From this, the only other reason I can think of to get drunk and pay for it with a hangover is the occasional tramp who claims he gets drunk with a Winter Westerner on the blow to sleep peaceably without frostbite.

I concur with most traditional treatments, however advise trying one at a time, as you concurrently distance from alcohol to avoid hangover. This single-variable approach is a controlled experiment to ferret out a Kure, and a standard medical technique.

As with any condition, first approach the *mechanism*—nuts and bolts—and proceed to the solution. Hangover causes dehydration because alcohol is a diuretic causing urination. So, dehydration is the target. Second, the metabolic breakdown products of alcohol are poisonous making one feel awful, so likewise they must be flushed out with copious water (distilled or spring). I believe teas and juices are a mistake for dehydration because one may not drink as many as good, pure water. My general rule is two day-after 12-ounce glasses of water per every one glass of night-before alcohol. That may take a couple of hours.

Preventive hydration *while* boozing, by drinking a glass of water for each glass of alcohol, is better. You won't get as drunk, and the hangover is cut perhaps in half.

Note: Those peanut shells strewn about the floor are the barkeep's keys to selling more drinks and hangovers asking for more analgesic shots. Instead, a stomach half-full of starches reduces absorption to slow the onset and reduce a hangover.

Significantly, drink a few glasses of water after a binge before going to bed to take the rough edges off the morning hangover. The nausea and vomiting are the irritating effect of alcohol on the stomach and intestinal linings, and touching the CNS. Flush these passages with water, for all linings are a second skin.

Preventive hydration while boozing by drinking a glass of water for each glass of alcohol is better. You won't get as drunk, and the hangover is cut perhaps in half.

A superior preventive is 'pre-fitness.' Champion athletes I've known in racquetball, handball, and track drank like sharks but owned splendid circulation and organs that spanked hangover poisons by the time they woke up from passing out. One Olympic miler asserts that he drank like a drunk but refused to be called one because he didn't really get high, never had a hangover, and one year quit cold turkey in a blink.

What's missed in conventional remedies is to stimulate circulation to speed natural metabolic breakdown of alcohol by exercising during a hangover. Walk off a hangover with a gallon jug of distilled water, sipping every few minutes. I've done this with miscellaneous toxicities.

We don't like to acknowledge, especially when having a good time, that alcohol is actually a drug. The body reacts as with any drug overdose, by metabolizing and getting rid of offending substances. The established cure is time, time for breakdown and excretion. Sleeping it off is not such a good habit to fall into, but having been orally poisoned a hundred times by other than alcohol, I know it works. The rest machinery enables the body to heal itself. I haven't popped an aspirin in decades, except for post-surgery pain, but it's a sound hangover analgesic. I prefer to pay the piper with brainless tasks around the homestead that involve movement as the body flushes the poison and a feeling of wellness slowly returns.

The best Kure for drinking—to keep drinking—is to earn each drop. A friend runs half a mile to merit each beer *before* the drink. A pre-paid mile per mixed drink is the tab, with no credit!

Are you an alcoholic? Alcoholics Anonymous (AA) works! I've seen too many success cases worldwide to think otherwise. Make an individualistic stab first, and then fall back on peers. The recovery caveat someone should tell AA clean-and-sobers is that he/she, rather than a faraway spirit influence, worked the cure… in order to avoid a nagging obligation. In Trinidad, I once met a charismatic ex-alcoholic and cocaine abuser who walked village to village helping others reach sobriety. He insisted, "When someone turns his life over to you to get clean-and-sober, you must rehearse each of his stages during a month of recovery to make it stick, and then congratulate him on getting well himself."

HEADACHES

What is it?

Call it migraine, tension, cluster or simple—it hurts. The causes are unknown or disputed, the symptoms are pressure and pain, and it's mistaken that 90% of all headaches are due to tension.

Traditional Treatment

Massage, a cool and quiet place, nap, distraction such as sport, biofeedback, relaxation training, over-the-counter pain relievers.

Kure

If necessity is the mother of invention, this is a case of a Kure being the offspring of headache. I developed a regimen during ages 8-20 that was so extensive I used to keep a list and check off the self-treatments one-at-a-time to ensure not one was missed.

Here's the list:

1. Endure while doing something enjoyable, such as a quiet walk, until it goes away.
2. Lie down where it's cool, for example, an air-conditioned room. Perhaps nap for thirty minutes.
3. Cover the eyes with blinders or the palms of the hands for five minutes.
4. Put an ice bag on the eyes and forehead.

5. Warm the hands by placing them in very warm water. I read this in a family-magazine column and was gratified by the instant result. In time, I learned to substitute gloves for water, which worked well in combination with ice on the eyes.
6. Massage the temples... self-administered or by someone else.
7. The head support. This one knocked my socks off, and I've been grateful to the student osteopath since the demonstration. He set me on the hard floor and supported the back of my head with his two index fingers, one each under the two occipital condyles. These bony projections at the back of the skull can be felt as hard bumps near the bottom just above the neck. With the weight of my head resting totally on his fingers, he said to close my eyes and relax for a couple minutes. In that time a severe headache drained away. I learned to do it myself with two fingers each under each condyle. There have been dozens of others on whom I've used the technique, often boasting that though the person may try to retain the headache, it would disappear in minutes. It worked 90 percent of the time! I suspect the mechanism has something to do with either a pressure point below the condyle, and/or in conjunction with pressing on the long neck

muscles that attach to those protuberances and tighten under tension.

8. Cold plunge or shower. I remember as my heart raced in glacier-like water that I would emerge clear-headed if only I could stay in for about three minutes. It worked.

9. Aspirin.

10. Throw in the towel and sleep for the night in a cool, quiet, dark place.

The treatments ran sequentially until success was had, and it was rare I reached number 7 before achieving a Kure. Note that aspirin was a last resort and once as a kennel-cleaning teen I went to the owner veterinarian and said, "I'm worried that I take too many aspirin." He looked concerned and asked how many. "Two a month," I said, and he replied that was not too many.

I reflect even now on the determination to conquer disease without opening a medicine cabinet. As a postscript, at age 30 the headaches fairly stopped. The reason is I made a conscious decision to rebuke them come Hades or high water, and it worked. I believe strong resolve should be reserved for rare instances in life, and I have no regret for having dropped headaches.

What is it?

Overheating to a severe degree. The internal heat regulators are overwhelmed so body temperature climbs to the height of a likely medical emergency. Shock, brain damage, kidney failure, coma, or death can result. The signs are body temperature over 104 degrees; headache‘ dizziness‘ confusion‘ hot, dry, and red skin; and profuse sweating initially followed by sweat shut-down, rapid breathing and heartbeat, and muscle cramps.

Traditional Treatment

Nearly every case is treated as an emergency and a professional sought. While waiting for help, the patient is moved to shade or an air-conditioned room, cooled with a wet sheet, reclined with feet elevated, fanned and given cool liquids.

Kure

The reality is that often no help is around when a person transitions from hyperthermia to heatstroke. Recently I hiked in the summer desert hills and became lost. After 20 hours and with all 3 liters of water gone, my tongue and oral cavity swelled and stuck together to impede breathing. I had to drink urine to open the airway. There was a GPS backup but it failed in this one instance; the second backup, a cell-phone, was useless because I had no voice. I was in mild heatstroke when the night's cool saved me. I walked all night to safety.

Super-hydrating is the preventive Kure for extreme exercise in a climate apt to bring heatstroke. My formula is to force-drink a pint each of distilled water, orange juice, milk, and Gatorade® before starting out. Wear a broad-brimmed hat. I concocted a double-hat for desert walking, in which one is placed atop the other, with about ½-inch space separating them. The top layer reflects the sun and the bottom holds sweat to act as a swamp cooler in a slight breeze. Douse the bottom one with water to enhance cooling. One key to hot weather hiking without overheating is to walk with your back to the sun, and save a downhill for the return trip. I walked the length of Death Valley as a childhood dream and found the going fine because my back was to the sun and it was winter months. In mid-trip I came across the bleaching bones of a hiker who apparently hadn't read the Kures, though I don't recall his orientation to the sun.

The bones of "Hank" were later recovered by park rangers, and RIP phoned by me to a sobbing daughter who had never even met dad.

The onset of heatstroke is insidious, like altitude sickness and scuba nitrogen narcosis. A fit person can march through the mild warning signs of dizziness and confusion only to collapse when in too deep a state of heatstroke. Once walking the hot length of Baja California, I didn't trust myself and constantly drank water, carrying a jug in each hand and more in the backpack causing me to urinate every 15 minutes. Monitor urine for frequency and color to develop a relationship to body hydration. If heatstroke strikes, follow the traditional treatment plus slowly drink the tepid Kure combination of water, juice, milk, and Gatorade.

In mid-trip I came across the bleaching bones of a hiker who apparently hadn't read the Kures, though I don't recall his orientation to the sun.

My remote desert trailer is along an illegal alien pipeline that runs from the Mexican border into California. One afternoon I returned to find a dozen illegal Mexicans collapsed in the shade of the trailer. Some were eating the inside of barrel cactus for moisture and others were passed out. They were hyperthermic and approaching heatstroke with rapid respiration and heart rate, headaches, stupor, and elevated body temperatures. But none thought it serious enough to want to call immigration and be shipped back to Mexico. I gave them liquids and shade, which is allowed by law, and saw them off to the North.

Humidity with heat brings heatstroke more quickly than heat alone, for the same reason that a steam bath heats you faster than a sauna. I overlooked this once on a summer distance run in Houston and went to the ground, but learned the reviving effect of alcohol rub and ice rub. Now I've developed a habit when overheated to head for the nearby cold Colorado River to soak for 10 minutes. Relief is quick, and a cold shower or bath work as well. The biggest tip to pass from experience is your body adapts to heat, as to other extremes. Take heat in small doses for two weeks before a full outing. Freeze two gallons of water and carry it, drinking the trickle. By the end of the hike or workday you'll feel refreshed.

What is it?

Also called piles, this is a ballooning of the network of veins under the mucous membrane and skin which lines the anal channel and anus. They can be thought of as varicose veins that cause itching, maybe bleeding, in the area. This is said to be an all-American condition, with one of every two people you see walking down the sidewalk developing them.

Traditional Treatment

Slim down, sit in hot water, soften your chair, soften the stool, keep the anus clean, exercise, defecate at initial urge, avoid constipation strain, lift heavy objects carefully. Also a high fiber diet, suppositories, itch ointment, drinking of fluids, and surgery.

Kure

I agree with the traditional treatments above. Try no more than one at a time and assay the result. Reuse the successes. This is called a controlled experiment, as opposed to simultaneously trying multiple variables and learning little. The condition has been studied from so many angles it would be difficult to come up with original Kures had not it been for Racquetball.

As a professional player, I matched strategy to opponent, and in one match I decided to take the legs out from under a player who was renowned for stamina, figuring then his game would collapse. It worked, and a few years later he approached me and said grimly, “In that match you ran me so hard I got horrid hemorrhoids. I’ve tried many treatments that don't work. You caused it, now can you fix it?" I felt so bad that I began a study of the subject, placing each new solution into a shoebox until I had enough to write an intelligent report to the sport. These are provided above in the conventional treatments, plus there are some originals below.

I suspect there is a secondary infection in many hemorrhoid conditions, especially those that bleed. A secondary infection means the inflamed anal tissue is more susceptible to bacteria. I disagree with the experts who advise avoiding soap at the anus since it irritates. Wash vigorously with lots of water and soap to cut the filth, then apply alcohol (and wait for the burn) or topical antibiotic. It is important to rub these in well (ref. "Cuts and Scrapes," page 27) because the heat and mechanical action carry the cream into the tissue, not just on top of it. You can sit on a heater or nearly on a candle to facilitate ointment penetration, and for relief.

I emphasize the importance of toning the anal veins to resist ballooning by practicing total body fitness. Additionally, remember that when you exercise you help hemorrhoids in two other ways: you'll drink more fluids and lose weight. Finally, I believe anal intercourse should be avoided in the hemorrhoid-ridden person. Someday someone may link bleeding hemorrhoids to anal intercourse to AIDS.

HYPOTHERMIA

What is it?

It is being cold, or medically speaking there is a drop in internal temperature to below normal. The lower the body core temperature, the more severe the effects. Normal body temperature is 98.6. Down to 94 degrees the heart rate slows and metabolism drops off, which brings shivering, numbness, and a grayish skin—uncomfortable but not serious for a healthy person. Below 94 degrees the speech slurs and thinking may be impaired with loss of consciousness. Wet or windy weather each doubles the severity of symptoms, by my estimation.

Traditional Treatment

Slowly rewarm with blankets and remember to cover the top of the head. Warm drinks may be given. Some folks prefer to have an ambulance called if mental alterations set in.

Kure

As with frostbite (ref. "Frostbite," page 31) my method of self-treatment includes three applications of warmth: external, internal, and through movement. The background for this is prodigious and I've met no one with broader, longer experience of hypothermia than yours truly. Moreover, there has never been a scenario I couldn't Kure hypothermia by gradually warming the outside body, slowly taking warm drinks, and moving. Both the "experts" and I agree that increasing body temperature by more than a couple degrees per hour is contraindicated in the elderly, and even uncomfortable for the fit and young.

My search-and-rescue instructors have always suggested skin-to-skin contact, and certainly recovery is more rapid than alone in a sleeping bag. One time on a freight train across rain-swept Nebraska a traveling companion, "ChooChoo" Chelsea, and I got in cold trouble. A sleeping bag blew overboard leaving us with a kids bag that the two of us couldn't fit in at the same time, but it opened at either end and we crawled in opposite ends with only our feet sticking out. The hypothermia passed, as, not too long after, did the relationship.

Dozens of terribly cold times have occurred in many countries, but I always knew that as long as I could walk and keep my head covered, I would live. Once on a southbound winter freight from Denver following the theft of my sleeping bag, I erred and hopped aboard a flatcar "on the fly" (as the train moved) because I wanted the ride badly. I was a healthy lad with a favorite sweatshirt that I figured would be sufficient protection for a few hours until the train reached lower and more southern regions. Nighttime came and proved overwhelming. I was unable to move around on the shuddering flatcar, so just sat and witnessed the onset of steps into hypothermia.

The hypothermia passed, as, not too long after, did the relationship.

This is what happened over the short time of an hour: Shaking, numbness, confusion, pain, and drifting into unconsciousness. The latter seemed welcome but I fought it in honor of Jack London's short story "To Build a Fire," in which the freezing protagonist never woke up and was eaten by wolves. After a couple hours the train sided in the mountains to allow another to pass. Unable to stand, I rolled off the car and onto the snowy ballast near the rail, and then crawled away from the wheels as the train started. I was lost in the mountains, but now I could move and begin the steps out of hypothermia. I belly crawled for five minutes, then on hands and knees for another five minutes, then managed a Frankenstein gait for the good part of an hour. I happened across a sheep manger with straw and fell to sleep. In the morning it was a new, sunny day and I walked out of the mountains.

Kures are better received from recovered survivors, so be assured that if you move to heat you'll weather almost any hypothermia.

INFECTIOUS MONONUCLEOSIS

What is it?

A viral infectious disease most often seen in people aged 10-35. It is generally not serious unless the spleen enlarges. Usual symptoms are a bad sore throat, swollen lymph nodes, possibly enlarged spleen, fever, weakness, headache, stiffness and other typical viral signs.

Traditional Treatment

Bed rest, fluids, aspirin, and gargle for the sore throat. Monitor spleen size. Expect to lie still for at least 2-3 weeks.

Kure

"You have the second worst case of mono in the history of San Diego County!" exclaimed Doc Hannah. "Get in bed." I was in the peak of health as a pro athlete, age 30, and the weakness, sore throat, and nausea hit me like a ton of bricks. I lay like a stone for a month and recall the number one radio tune was "There's Got to Be a Morning After." Quick in, faster out is a medical adage, and one day I woke up, ate three breakfasts and was healed.

The lessons from this experience are hard-hitting:

- ☐ Diagnosis—a sore throat with weakness and enlarged spleen are clues of mononucleosis.
- ☐ Treatment—stay in bed two more days after you feel like getting out. If the spleen (right lower abdomen) hurts or feels bigger to the touch, consult a doctor.

- ☐ Aftermath—relapse is a distinct possibility that some doctors underplay.

In my case, I felt like entering tournaments immediately but my sports medicine doctor stepped in and said, wait another month, and drink great volumes of good liquids through recovery.

> *"You have the second-worst case of mono in the history of San Diego County!"*

LICE

What is it?

Lice are small, gray, wingless bugs that crawl on the body and feed on blood. There are head, pubic (crabs), and body lice. Females lay eggs (nits) and these, or the insect itself, are spread by direct contact or via clothes. The itch and scratching may cause a secondary skin infection.

Traditional Treatment

Prevent by cleanliness, washing clothes, and checking for nits in pubic and head hair. Avoid sharing clothes, hats, and combs. Treatment is fairly straightforward and lice usually don't pose a health hazard beyond nuisance. Many over-the-counter body lotions and shampoos work well.

Kure

The lice pros forget to emphasize the mechanism of the killing cream on the skin or hair. Rub in well for a minute, leave it on for generally 12 hours. Stay naked with the lotion on if possible. Reapply if you sweat, bathe, or workout. After the suggested time, it's important to wash with hot water to get rid of the lotion, dead insects, and nits, too. In the case of scalp lice, massage the shampoo into the scalp, then leave on twice as long as recommended. Read about the fascinating life cycle of lice to understand the importance of changing clothes and laundering daily in hot water. Exercise often and drink plenty of fluids to promote vitality and reverse any toxic effects of the lotion.

It is common in Third World countries to see families on the porch picking nits from each other's scalps. And in a college hobo class I once taught, we tried the same, though none were found. Some missions I frequent while vagabonding require a preliminary "bug check," which is a diagnostic ultraviolet light shined on the crotch and head. One nit and you get the bum's rush. True hobos, who ride the rails and usually eschew missions, sleep outdoors and have their own Kures. I have seen them "boiling up" their clothes in camps to kill the "gray soldiers". They carry urinal soap in a pocket to stay lice-free. Herbal pharmacies also offer sweet flag and turmeric as pediculicides (lice killers).

You may also effectively shave the area, as evidenced by a distraught friend who returned home to find his wife had left him. He shaved one half—the left side—of his beard and kept it shaved, along with the lice, until she returned.

What is it?

An infection common in New England caused by a bacterium that is carried from mice or deer to people. Animals remain asymptomatic (no disease) except humans who may display the diagnostic bullseye at bite site within 30 days. This is a red rash with a pale center; the bite lesion (small, red, and flat or raised) lies in dead center. Flu-like symptoms may occur in that month, while in the ensuing two years a preponderance of reports of other complaints materialize, including joint problems. Not everyone is susceptible to the disease, there is little chance of infection if the tick is removed within a day after attachment, and even for those who contract Lyme disease spontaneous remission often occurs.

Traditional Treatment

Tick check and removal, treat the symptoms, use of antibiotics and pain relievers.

Kure

The pillars of this disease, including diagnosis, testing, symptoms, and treatment, in my opinion are inconclusive yet breed New England paranoia. I lived and hiked daily in tick-infested Connecticut woods that crawled with mice and deer. I picked tiny "deer ticks" off the neighborhood kids, dogs, and myself regularly. This tick-picking is key to prevention of the disease.

At a catered dinner table where I sat, the host turned to his wife and said, "Dear, is that a tick on the cheek?" She replied, "Yes, dear, shall I get the tick kit?" She did and we were entertained. He didn't develop any symptoms, but one day I met a woodsman who did. He had displayed the typical three-inch red bulls-eye around the bite, developed some flu signs, then joint pain, and was successfully treated with antibiotics.

> *... ticks should be removed, and I disagree that one cannot be removed with head intact using petroleum jelly smear or a blown-out match on its butt....*

Remember that not all ticks cause Lyme disease, and even among the correct ticks only 20-60 percent carry the bacteria. Even then, many people who are bitten don't contract the disease. I don't let it keep me out of the woods, and would volunteer as a guinea pig if it would have statistical impact. Of course, ticks should be removed and I disagree that one cannot be removed with head intact using petroleum jelly smear or a blown-out match on its butt (though the pro tick kit with curved tweezers and integral magnifier is better). Mind where you toss the tick. I drink lots of fluids and move around for a day after taking off a tick. New Englanders will dispute it, but I think Lyme disease is a compromised-host project of nature: If you stay in shape with accompanying excellent circulation and lymph systems you'll stay safe in the forest.

MUSCLE CRAMP

What is it?

Painful tightening of a muscle from extended use, dehydration, and electrolyte depletion. An injury may also trigger the cramp or, rarer, a systemic problem such as diabetes. Most athletes experience a cramp sooner or later and rise to compete again.

Traditional Treatment

Ice the cramp and take fluids and electrolytes. for example, via a sport drink. Stretch the cramped muscle and massage. Pinch the upper lip. Quinine with doctor's approval.

Kure

Crying, like pinching the lip, distracts and often lets the cramped muscle relax, as I personally attest. I like ice on the spasm for the first hour while keeping the muscle in a stretched position and sipping constantly from tepid (not cold) electrolyte replacement drink.

Note: Any sport drink should be diluted 1:1 with water, whether used for prevention, enjoyment, or treatment.

If you have a cramp-prone muscle, stretch it before and during exercise and keep it warm and out of drafts during a rest or timeout. The adage "drink before you get thirsty and rest before you get tired" is prudent.

In sports contests there may be no time to rest. I used to forestall cramps on the racquetball pro circuit by voluminous prehydration, plus a game strategy that used rally-ending "kill shots" to shorten matches. Nonetheless, I succumbed to cramps a dozen times. The worst was at a Patterson, New Jersey, tournament where I entered two events, singles and doubles, and worked to the finals in both.[1]

The cramps started on the plane trip home, and the two large trophies on either seat beside me were no help. I fastened the seat belt and both hands tightened. I raised my eyes in surprise and both lids cramped. Trying to relax, I tilted my head back and the throat contracted. Then other muscle groups went and I could do nothing but stare. This was an extreme case due to typical causes, along with the plane air conditioning. I sat it out and by the time the plane landed in Detroit had recovered all but the legs, which returned the next day.

I've experimented thoroughly with leg cramps of the quads, hamstrings, and calves. Mental control plays a role, but stretching, warmth, and liquids before and during extended workouts are better. You can "run

---

[1] The author's professional racquetball career paralleled the sport's evolution during the 1970s and 1980s. He wrote the 'bible,' *Complete Book of Racquetball*, and opened racquetball doors in every state, and Central and South America, with hundreds of clinics and exhibitions. Keeley developed into a stroke and strategy trendsetter featured in *Sports Illustrated* ('He Found His Racquet,' Nov. 19, 1979).

through" a cramp as I did in a marathon, but it has a possible steep downside of permanent injury, so be careful. In the particular race, the leg tied up at about the ten-mile mark, then was okay by the 20-mile mark. However, once I tried to bicycle through a calf cramp on a trip between Canada and Mexico, and I still occasionally pay for it. If possible, stop and treat a cramp immediately. When icing skin, either move the cold around or pack it in a cloth. A night's rest and slow return to activity works almost every time for a muscle cramp.

Less serious is the related occupational cramp. These come from turning a wrench, writing, painting or typing, woe if a boss notices a slow-down. The contracting muscles are smaller, so less painful, and the Kures are the same as other cramps. Instead of a coffee break, take a sport drink one.

What is it?

It hits nearly everyone sometime and the symptoms include a sharp pain, tingling, ache, or just the stiffness. There may be a grating sensation upon head rotation and a shooting sensation down the back or arm. You can wake up with a stiff neck, play sports and suffer it, or suffer a blow from an accident.

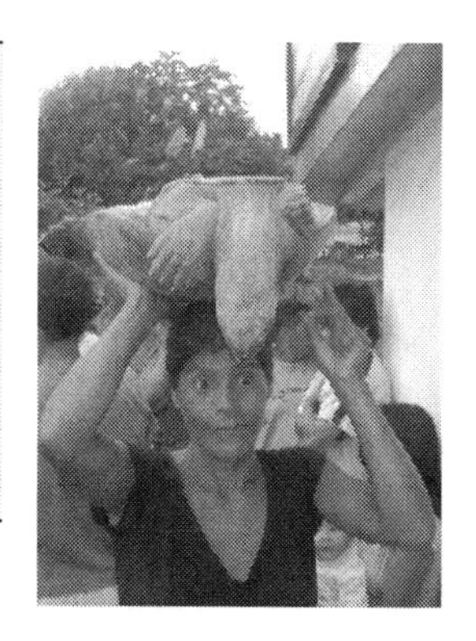

Traditional Treatment

Apply cold during the first day, and heat thereafter. Stretch and exercise the neck. Rub in topical ointment to alleviate pain and inflammation. Visit the doctor if it persists or is accompanied by fever or swollen lymph nodes.

Kure

The methods above reflect those I used for years as a wrestler; however, I devised more. Cold treatment in the form of ice within a cloth is crucial for swelling in the first 24 hours. At night, sleep with a long towel or sweatshirt around your neck for warmth. Sleep on your back without a pillow other than maybe a heating pad under the neck. A waterbed helps. A cold draft on the neck *anytime* should be avoided.

From here on, the Kures become strange and proportionally effective. If one doesn't get the stiff neck from sports, arthritis, or accident, the likely cause is overuse at the computer, TV, or from reading. The mechanics of these is that if you take any joint, put it at an odd tilt, and hold it there long enough, there'll be stiffness. The head sits like a bowling ball atop the shoulders and is attached by the neck muscles. Most computer monitors are mounted lower than the nose and this makes the head roll forward on its stalk. This brings the muscles in the back of the neck into play to keep it from rolling forward, and after a few hours results in pain or stiffness. The correction is so simple as to be laughable. Raise the computer screen with books, wood or bricks so the midpoint is eye-level or slightly higher. There is instant relief, as well as prevention all at once.

From here on, the Kures become strange and proportionally effective. If one doesn't get the stiff neck from sports, arthritis, or accident, the likely cause is overuse at the computer, TV, or from reading.

I once spent a year at the computer, eight hours a day seven days a week, typing an autobiography. My endurance was tripled by raising the screen and doubled again by turning the monitor upside down (ref. "Vision Problems," page 91). The idea is that words and sentences flow from left to right (unless Hebrew, Arabic, Japanese, or Chinese) and the body, especially the back and neck, "sets" to receive the images as if preparing for little blows. When you turn the monitor upside down, the words flow in the opposite direction to allow the eyes, neck and back to set in another way. Similarly, if you read many books, learn to turn the book upside down and read from bottom to top, right to left. I've tested this on people with eye, neck and back problems to great satisfaction. You could also give "mirror writing" a try. TV-watching heads should put the screen just above eye level.

Massage and exercising the neck help in recovery. I developed a sequence of neck rotations, flexions, and extensions that are easily copied from the imagination. Analgesic heating ointments work but fall short unless rubbed in well for a minute. I have a theory that some chronic stiffs are the result of poor vision; if you suspect this, fit yourself with a pair of nonprescription reading glasses from a pharmacy or see an ophthalmologist.

OBESITY

What is it?

Obesity is when you look in the mirror and think you weigh too much. It's been defined as a weight of more than 20% above what is considered normal for a body mass index based on age, height, and so forth, that may be found online. Simply, you carry more and larger fat cells throughout the body, with distasteful results.

Traditional Treatment

Diets, fasts, clubs, doctors explaining it's not your fault, eating more in a vicious circle of being unhappy from being fat, acupuncture, behavior modification... *ad nauseam.*

Kure

You don't need a doctor to inform you that you're overweight, or a psychologist to instruct you to lose weight—just Kures. I used to Paparazzi fat friends and quietly tape photos on their bathroom scales as their blackball doctor *and* psychologist. It worked. The first step to shed pounds is with resolve off the scale—and half the battle is won. Then, in the first week of discomfort as ounces melt off, tell yourself repeatedly, "It gets easier." It does; take it from a peer.

My life goals have revolved around food reward since getting no seconds as an active kid edging up to the table, and later cutting weight for high school wrestling. In college, during physiology and nutrition classes, they tagged me Breadman for sneaking a dozen rolls from the dorm kitchen after each meal for calories to compete in dog-eat-dog veterinary school. I slipped the dorm to join Farmhouse Fraternity of hefty overall geniuses because the feed was *ad libitum* (at one's pleasure). In a week the cook named the garbage disposal "Keeley," a tribute.

I read James Clavell's *Noble House* and was inspired by a few castaways in a hungry pit to stop eating for a week while endeavoring to maintain a daily routine of work and running six miles. There never was a more appreciated carrot at the other end. Then I flip-flopped, telling people, "How can I instruct others to lose weight until I've been obese?" Harder than dieting, I shot up 40 lb., to 200 lb., and gently dieted back down.

Besides starting now, and reminding yourself it's going to get easier, the following 10 steps distill the lessons for keeping your weight right:

1. Eat everything you want, but cut out sugar, desserts, and bread.
2. Eat any quantity you wish, if you will block off one or two hours a day for exercise.
3. Don't look at the scale during the first week, and thereafter only once a week during the first month. This helps prevent thinking about food.
4. You are fat, so perhaps don't deserve this: limit weight loss to two pounds a week, or less. The rationale approximates the slow growth of a healthy small business, for similar reasons.

5. When you reach a goal of, say, a 20 lb. loss, *don't* celebrate, unless it's by maintaining a lifelong commitment to strong diet.
6. Put a lock on the refrigerator. This is the best advice you'll ever get, because if you can't get to the food you feel less hungry not thinking about accessibility. A pantry corollary is stocked only with healthful food. You also may dramatically relocate to where there's less food, or try the "Boxcar Diet:" a favorite of chunky hoboettes hopping freights with long hours of vibration along the rails, and walking endless tracks between chow.
7. You may join a weight loss club or enlist a fan club for encouragement, although an individualistic effort yields lifelong comprehensive rewards… viz the fire walking experience.
8. I've fasted via many trials on the trails that boil down to eating fewer poor foods, more healthy food, and exercise. Hence, diet is the simple math of negating calories: Put less in one end than the sum of metabolic processes and what comes out the other end. It's guaranteed.
9. A novel route to thinness is a long hike, e.g. along the Pacific or Appalachian trails. In a month, you won't recognize your reflection in a clear pool.

10. The best tidbit, in a moment of indecision over the Good Menu, is drink a glass of water before a treat, and the hunger vanishes.

These are ten tips to skinny down. If the flab won't fall off after a month of proper food, exercise, and Kures, see a physician to diagnose a metabolic problem that hinders weight loss in perhaps 1 in 1000 people.

PSORIASIS

What is it?

A common skin condition that shows in itching red patches on any part of the body, though most frequently on the knees, elbows, or scalp. The rash consists of raised, red bumps covered with whiter, flaking scales. In affected areas, new skin cells are produced at an accelerated rate and work their way to the outermost layer, where they accumulate to cause the ailment. General health is normally not altered, however the unsightly patches are tenacious and potentially embarrassing. The cause is unknown, though stress has been suggested as playing a part.

Traditional Treatment

Practice cleanliness. Use moisturizing creams for dryness, controlled ultraviolet light, mineral salt baths, vitamin A topically and orally, and apply symptomatic treatments for the itching.

Kure

For prevention, I believe a person who relaxes daily is less prone to psoriasis. A fit person who eats well, drinks good water (ref. the water discussion in "Bladder Stones," page 12) and exercises daily should never need worry about it. For treatment, I suggest strong exercise and especially swimming. Understand that raised heart rate during physical movement increases circulation through the skin and underlying tissues, which promotes healing. Outdoor exposure to sunlight and air is beneficial. I concur with vitamin A therapy without going overboard, but if taken orally precede this and any medication with a glass of water before and another after. Eat well and consider becoming a vegetarian. Wear no clothes over the rash, and try to find a hot spring to soak in.

A rare date visited my far-flung desert trailer last year and was shy about showing her legs. "I have psoriasis that won't go away," she told me. She acknowledged that stress multiplied the condition and Benadryl® relieved it. (Benadryl is a popular medication for sensitivity or allergic reactions.) I told her to walk down to the wash (a dry, sandy riverbed), take off her clothes, put a layer of clean, white sand on the patches and sit in the sun for an hour. She returned in smiles and with hardly an itch, for the condition had abated by half. Next I went up the hill to a desert family for advice.

"Why," the lady of the house said, "I was just bitten by our pet scorpion and have some Benadryl I'd be happy to give." She produced a baggy with a small amount of ointment that had melted in the heat. My date applied it in the convenient prewarmed form (ref. the heating and rubbing ointment comments in "Cuts and Scrapes," page 27) and found even greater relief. After three days of the repeated regimen, the skin had healed well and she returned to civilization.

RUNNER'S KNEE (ATHLETIC KNEE ISSUES)

What is it?

Pain at the front one or both knees, sometimes with inflammation. Actually a small sprain of the knee ligaments caused by overuse rather than sudden trauma. The condition is fairly common in varying degrees among joggers.

Traditional Treatment

Initial diagnosis is on the basis of discomfort. Most knee conditions respond to rest with hot or cold pack treatment. Another activity should be engaged for a few weeks to prevent recurrence. In moderate cases, mobility may be hampered by swelling, but in severe instances cartilage may tear and cause the knee to lock up and a doctor should be sought. aspirin or anti-inflammatories may be used. Athletes find the symptoms more a nuisance than permanent.

Kure

This entry deals narrowly with overuse by the runner or athlete. I have seen it often, suffered it occasionally, and treated it with satisfaction. Prevention begins with the shoe, and the air soles work well. Consider a quality insole for this jarring injury. Moreover, try two insoles per shoe. Running or working surface is as important as the shoe. I never had the symptoms while running for five years on the "hard sands" of high tide along the California coast, but the old injury would flare on pavement. Dirt roads make a fine surface. If you run a track, circle in the opposite direction and feel the relief, usually, provided to the outside leg and knee which is allowed a longer stride.

Once I ran 100 laps around an indoor eighth-mile track to prove the point. The traditional treatment of switching to an alternate sport is both sound and underrated. Stick with the other activity until symptoms abate, plus at least two weeks. A similar program is alternating sports by the week, running for one, bicycling the next, swimming the third, and so on. Finally, there is the "run through the pain" course as advocated by my former cross-country coach. I once did this in a marathon and the pain disappeared at mile twenty, but this is not something I recommend.

My proudest discovery used to be outlandish: walking and running backward. Today, track coaches realize that quadriceps (front) muscle tears on sprinters can be prevented by having them sprint backward to strengthen the hamstring (rear) muscles. The practice stabilizes the knee to avoid sprain. Once I jogged backward for an hour on a treadmill and rather than feel knee pain, it subsided.

There are other exercises such as leg "crossovers," "kangaroo hops" and "monster walks" (taking large steps while bending the knee), as well as exercises with weights. From a lifetime of and recovery from mild knee injuries, I use and suggest ankle weights for knee strength and stability at home, at the work place, and in the sports field. Use them before injury for prevention, or during rehabilitation… after there is no more pain or swelling.

Ice or heat? Apply ice to swelling during the first 24 hours, especially in the first hour. I don't use ice except for pain. Wrap the ice in a pillowcase or towel. My habit is take sports injury to the pool where flutter kicking using a kickboard or while holding the poolside builds strength, endurance, and flexibility. I once invented underwater racquetball, using a lightly weighted ball and scuba gear. I've also done sprints in water, but it requires waist or ankle weights to keep from floating. Surf running in a foot of water builds tremendous legs. Racehorses train underwater with heads out, and I foresee the same for two-legged athletes. There will be gyms underwater to the shoulders until space exploration takes us to Jupiter where its tremendous gravity will provide the training grounds for champions.

Racehorses train underwater with heads out, and I foresee the same for two-legged athletes.

Once I went to a doctor for a job physical and noticed him limping. He was a triathlete and had a sore, swollen knee from running and working. "Let me tell you five things about knee injuries your doctor won't tell you," I said, and proceeded:

1. Switch to bicycling until the inflammation goes away.
2. Run on nothing harder than dirt.
3. Start backward walking and running.
4. Sleep on your back with the knee elevated.

5. After recovery wear ankle weights around the office. I tapped my own weights and said to check with me in two weeks.

What is it?

This entry describes a bite from a venomous snake, as opposed to a nonvenomous one which usually can be treated as a simple wound or animal bite. A poisonous snakebite is always serious, yet unless the victim is a child, elderly or infirm, death is unlikely.

Traditional Treatment

Modern advice is to seek medical attention immediately. First aid is to place the bitten area (usually a hand or leg) lower than the rest of the body, immobilize it with a board splint, and some authorities allow application of ice. Some suggest capturing the snake for identification.

Kure

One familiar with past decades of recommended snakebite procedure averages the sum and comes up confused. Modern experts say sit and wait for help, as if bites happen at the supermarket vegetable stand. Bitten folks tell me walk to safety if the wound's on the hand, or play wait-and-see if on the leg. Factors that come into play include fitness, distance to vehicle, availability of shelter, food and water, plus size and type of the poison bolus (a rounded mass, the size of a pea for a Western diamondback).

There are four venomous snakes in this country—rattlesnake, coral, copperhead, water moccasin—and I'm pleased to have encountered them all in the wild. I'm most familiar with the western diamondback rattler, which I've jumped, skirted, and stoned to scare about 120 times. Yet I maintain respect for it, and one time after walking 600 miles through Baja California I chose to turn back just short of the goal because the rattlers got too thick.

Humans appear large to American snakes, and I've never had one chase me, nor have I heard a reliable account of that happening. The meanest looking snake I ever saw was a water moccasin while on a walk the length of Florida. He had a brow like an ex-con, was four feet long, and peered menacingly through raindrops as I dipped into his guarded pool for. He held his ground, as snakes will, but didn't attack. However, had I had fish breath or been carrying a fresh catch he would have been in my face because that is his daily fare.

My Kure procedure was developed after I understood the idea of a bolus of poison lying in the tissue and the desirability of stalling its absorption and transport to the heart, lungs, and brain. I carry a suction Extractor® available at outfitting stores that creates a vacuum to draw the poison. My mental rehearsal for a venomous bite is this: Apply the extractor, a suction cup, or suck the poison out by mouth. Visualize the bolus as the size of, say, a pea and assume it stays firm in the tissue for about a minute (depending on the type of venom and site puncture) before being absorbed into the blood. I personally use a tourniquet as once taught in Boy Scouts and Red Cross first aid, but authorities now discourage its use. After suctioning, I apply ice to reduce circulation from the wound toward the heart, and I keep the bitten appendage lower than the rest of the body for the same reason

Some desert folks where I live catch rattlers by hand, but the most prolific was Butch, my San Diego Swap Meet mentor. He displays scars of a half-dozen bites on his left arm, as his technique is to distract with the left and grab behind the head with the right. He says that after each bite the arm swelled painfully, he iced it, lowered it, took aspirin for pain and after a nauseating night felt fine. The point is to discourage snake catching while reversing the poppycock about aggressiveness of American snakes and their bites.

If you enter foreign jungles, be careful because snakes there grow bigger and great care is in order. My Peruvian guide was hired to shoot one that was bothering a village. He found the snake partially coiled on the ground and 45 feet long, looking down on him. He fired a shotgun blast from ten yards into the ear and it chased him through the jungle, knocking down small trees for a hundred yards before it expired. On one occasion in India, I was nose to nose with a 10-foot black cobra rising out a charmer's basket. The man motioned with his flute that I could pet the snake so I did on top the head. It nudged my hand affectionately like a poodle, however it was stupid of me in the first place and I plan never to repeat the risk (ref. "Travel Fatigue," page 88).

Two rattlesnake bite victims reported to me that they were rushed to the hospital and given antivenin. The trick is to give the antivenin *intramuscularly*. One of them didn't know this, nor did his doctor, and seconds after the intravenous drip began he was "code blue" with a stopped heart. The other victim did know this but his ignored words before going code blue were, "Not intravenously!" Both were revived and billed for cardiac arrest. Certainly a hospital or doctor's office is the place to be five minutes after a venomous bite, but it's prudent to know the Kures, too.

On one occasion in India, I was nose to nose with a 10-foot black cobra rising out a charmer's basket.

SPRAINS AND STRAINS

What is it?

A sprain is an injury to a ligament (attaches bone to bone), while a strain usually refers to an injury of a tendon (attaches muscle to bone). Either happens most often when twisting occurs at a joint such as the foot or wrist that makes little tears in the ligament or tendon. Pain and swelling happen, and sometimes a bruise and redness.

Traditional Treatment

Most sprains and strains are mild to moderate and disappear in a few days by treating with cold packs and keeping weight off the affected joint. Most problems are treated at home through RICE (acronym for rest, ice, compression, and elevation). Some people favor over-the-counter analgesics. If the condition lingers with pain, characterized by a marked joint immobility or an increasing swelling, then a doctor is consulted.

Kure

Much to add here: It is imperative to elevate and ice immediately following the injury before swelling becomes extensive. The most popular sprain is the ankle. It should be wrapped in towel-covered ice and raised a bit above the leg to beg the aid of gravity. Stay this way at least 30 minutes. Continue the 30-minute sessions at 3-hour intervals until most of the swelling is gone. Discontinue the icing sequence at night but sleep with the injured spot raised. It's likely you'll wake with a normal looking joint the next morning, but proceed with caution.

Now comes a transition period during treatment that is an art among veterinarians accustomed to horse lameness. Their—and human medicine's—historic controversy about the application of cold, heat, or alternating cold/heat may be distilled to this: Apply cold for the first 24 hours or until the swelling is gone, but never heat. After the first 24 hours, and especially if the swelling is gone, apply nothing or warmth. In 2-3 days, consider alternating heat-cold treatments with 15-minutes of heat, immediately followed by 15-minutes of cold, spaced apart about three times a day. The idea is to stimulate circulation as well as avoid swelling. During those 2-3 days continue to elevate the affected limb at night, and keep it warm. Wear a sock or mitten on an injured foot or hand at night, but it must fit loosely.

My baptism to sprains/strains came in college paddleball with a sudden badly twisted ankle. The recovery was routine over a couple of days, and I was back on the court again. Over the next two years in the sport of fast starts-and-stops I repeated the sprain in both feet a dozen times and was guided to my own methods. I found a Kure in hi-top tennis shoes, after which there was hardly a recurrence. Hi-tops with canvas uppers add tremendous ankle support. My choice was the Converse brand because I wore different colored shoes on each foot to display individuality and the company offered a crayon box selection. Later they sponsored me.

Note that the acronym RICE (rest, ice, compression, and elevation) is excellent for the initial golden 24 hours. But after the swelling and pain are out, my conviction is gently to move the joint to provide circulation to the area and to prevent it from stiffening. Easy sessions of walking, swimming, or biking are fine. If the swelling persists, my experience suggests to visit a sports medicine doctor rather than a regular MD. When I was 25 my regular doctor told me that because of past injuries I had the body of a 40-year-old. When I was beyond 40, my sports medicine doctor said that because of my active life I had the body of a 25-year-old.

As with other musculoskeletal problems, start with the most conservative treatment and progress to the more dramatic. I disfavor painkillers and anti-inflammatories other than aspirin for mild injuries. Temporary braces are okay but catch them if they become a mental crutch.

STROKE

What is it?

An obstruction of an artery carrying blood (with oxygen) to the brain, or the rupture of one of the cerebral arteries. The brain's requirement for oxygen is cut off with the result of a sudden, severe headache. There may be weakness or paralysis on one or both sides of the face or body. The legs may tingle and become numb. The signs of stroke have much to do with the severity. Stroke may also be accompanied by speech and swallowing difficulty, nausea, vomiting, vision abnormality, dizziness, confusion, memory loss, and unconsciousness.

Traditional Treatment

No cure exists, and two-thirds of cases result in permanent disability. Strokes are the third leading cause of death in America. Prevention is the key.

Kure

A Kure, however, does exist. To a degree. First, I agree with prevention because a stroke is like getting hit by a tank, and it's best to get out of the way. Picture arteries in the skull as thin convoluted straws that carry oxygen in solution to the brain. These can be kept clean and open by proper diet and exercise. Food that is low in fat, cholesterol and salt keeps the arteries from narrowing. Exercise builds blood-vessel integrity. Drink good water rather than from the tap (ref. the discussion of water in "Bladder Stones," page 12).

Lose weight, if needed, so the heart doesn't have to pump so hard. If you don't like the idea of delayed gratification then statistically you'll be a risk to join the aforementioned two-thirds.

Put aside a block of the day for relaxing (ref. discussion on life's priorities in "Anxiety Attacks," page 6). Hypertension is the greatest risk factor with stroke. The simple mechanics in my mind are that when the body "revs" continually it begins to accept high stress as the normal state. The pressure of blood against its vessel walls is harder, and the chance of rupture increases. Besides stress, continual use of caffeine, tobacco, and cocaine or amphetamine raises blood pressure. If regular periods of winding down can be arranged, blood pressure decreases and the chance of stroke diminishes

> *The greatest healer of disease is a recovered peer.... I've contracted and shrugged half the diseases in the Merck Manual, including stroke.*

At a relatively young age I had one of the more severe strokes I've read about. It was a painful learning trip to Hades for a few minutes until paralysis took over. I think respiration shut down until I lost consciousness. The next day I was surprised my timbers hadn't been shivered permanently, and attributed it to being fit, albeit overworked. The first week of recovery I chose to spend in solitary without conventional malarkey. I drank lots of liquid, walked great distances daily, and found quiet places to read. I didn't watch television or read the newspaper.

Within a week all dizziness and uncoordination was gone, never to return. I went on to explore life as fully as before.

If you have a family history of stroke or high blood pressure, or are unable to switch at will into a lower mental gear, then look now to exercise, food, and relaxation to pave your future well being. I used to work in an old folk's home where I learned much of courage in stroke management. One old–timer remarked, "Listen here, sonny. This ain't a dress rehearsal. Live and live well." The greatest healer of disease is a recovered peer, and hence the value of this book. I've personally contracted and shrugged off half the diseases in the *Merck Medical Manual*, including stroke.

Temporomandibular Joint Syndrome (TMJ)

What is it?

Pain and inflammation in the joint where the upper sides of the lower jaw hook to the skull. It's curiously more prevalent in women. Tendons and ligaments that hold the jaw in place normally work smoothly, but with the condition there is a painful uncoordination during eating, speaking, and other activities. The claims for cause include grinding the teeth for whatever reason, improper teeth alignment, eating chewy food, and whiplash or a blow to the jaw. In more serious cases there can be swelling at the joint, a clicking or popping noise, a locked jaw, headaches, earaches, and secondary muscle pains in the neck, shoulders. or back.

Traditional Treatment

Common sense attempts include hot and cold packs, eschewing chewy food, the conscious halt of teeth grind, stress avoidance, dental assistance or surgery, and tranquilizers or pain relievers.

Kure

This ailment has irritated me on three separate occasions: One time from chewing sticky candy too long, another from going into solitude only to return and talk too much all at once and strain the jaw, and the third time when struck in face. The TMJ sensation is distantly painful but mostly irritating. In one of the instances I got jaw 'clicks' and that's when I decided TMJ was simply a sprained or strained jaw. The conventional cures do well but are incomplete. My technique on two occasions was to give the face an overall rest and sleep warmly on my back without a pillow. The symptoms remitted in two days. The third case was tenacious and after a month I visited an orthodontist… who ground my teeth to perfectly expensive alignment, that was ineffective. That's when I gave serious consideration to TMJ and compassion to the hundreds of thousands of sufferers.

Let's start Kures with the wisdom teeth and admit that perfunctorily pulling them is a money-making machine for dentists and a direct cause of TMJ. Of course, veterinarians have parallels in their pet array of inoculations, and MDs with yearly physicals for the healthy, so I'm not picking on any one professional. I had mine routinely yanked at a young age for the usual poppycock reasons. Keep your wisdoms if your dentist gives you a choice. The reason is they are the large rear part of the platform interface between the lower and upper jaws, which is where TMJ occurs.

… after a month, I visited an orthodontist who ground my teeth to perfectly expensive alignment, that was ineffective.

Grinding teeth is probably for the same reason folks bite their nails: noise. Chronic TMJ victims should shy away from the stress of noise and its facial ramifications. Sleep quietly on your back without a pillow so the jaw falls back into a more restful, natural position. Chiropractors may suggest poor posture as leading to TMJ *a la* thrusting the chin forward, but they forget this also takes place if you sleep on your stomach. People who say they can't stop talking, and have TMJ, have likely self-diagnosed the cause and Kure.

Finally, I developed some preventive jaw exercises for myself that are easily explained by pressing the lower jaw against a resistance to the side and downward directions. I expect general fitness to cut the incidence of TMJ in half, as with any other joint sprain or strain. I finally got rid of my worst case with these methods, combined with eating nothing but soft foods for two weeks.

TICS

What is it?

Involuntary, quick, repeated movements (or less frequently vocalization) of unknown cause, ranging in severity, and of varying duration. The tics usually involve muscle groups in the face or shoulders and arms, though they can be elsewhere. Some common cases include multiple blinking, raising the eyebrow or forehead, mouth-corner twitching, head turning, shoulder shrugs, facial grimace and leg kicks. Psychologists are fond of pointing to accompanying behavioral disturbances.

Traditional Treatment

The cause of simple tics is said to be mysterious, giving the pros little to build on. Most simple tics spontaneously disappear in a year or so without treatment. Behavioral therapy is used, or drugs in extreme cases.

Kure

Knowing the mechanism is important in disease treatment because if one identifies the cause and removes it then usually the disease no longer exists. My idea is that in a simple tic there is a nerve and a muscle involved in a vicious loop of mutual stimulation, leading to a refiring nerve and an inflamed muscle. Which comes first, the nerve or the muscle? It can be either, and if one can be corrected the tic disappears. The question becomes how to bring to rest one or the other.

Treatment requires getting at the tic from inside and out, and it can take weeks or months to heal. General exercise accomplishes the inside job by continuously changing the "bathwater" in which nerve and inflamed muscle sit. Specific exercising of the tic muscles warm it and produce a "memory" that eventually lets the area relax. Good diet and especially (good) water (ref. discussion on water in "Bladder Stones," page 12) must be taken. Massage the affected area twice a day.

Which comes first, the nerve or the muscle? It can be either, and if one can be corrected the tic disappears.

The next idea is offbeat, but I've used it regularly in sports to success. Any body movement can be performed by any of a number of muscle groups. Take the simple act of raising the hand over the head—there are many muscle groups to choose from to orchestrate this. I think the best way to move—from walking to throwing a baseball—is to use the smallest muscle group that is closest to the point of action. The application to tics is simple. One muscle or muscle group produces a tic, yet other nondiseased muscles can take over the same movement as the tic. Learn those other groups by practice and feel, or view an anatomical chart (*Gray's Anatomy* is a classic), and use them to give the tic a chance to rest and heal.

A place exists for will power, therefore for behavioral training, in this condition. I once experimented with blinking for a month, attempting to stop. The blink has been said to be a natural tic. I succeeded for periods of up to an hour, then usually slipped, but am convinced that with fuller attention better results can be had. A tic victim can concentrate in similar ways to free himself.

One finds more will power in times of less stress, and thus by simplifying, slowing, and quieting, the condition may self-correct. Sleep with the affected area in a relaxed position that mildly stretches the associated muscles. Consider earplugs and nightshades. Warm it all night. The tic Kure has no room for tobacco or caffeine. Perhaps decrease some routine satisfactions but continue to work out at the gym or track.

What is it?

A low energy condition that may accompany travel. The primary symptoms are not serious but can sour vacation fun or undermine business efficiency. Headache, nausea, and/or decreased mental performance typically occur. No infectious agent has been identified, though being compromised can allow a secondary condition such as a cold to take hold. The condition usually disappears within a couple of days after return to home port.

Traditional Treatment

Prevention includes being rested before travel, being fit, drinking liquids before departure, and relaxing. Treatment is symptomatic for nausea, headaches, with a possible alcoholic drink or tranquilizer. Good sleep during travel is essential, as is proper food and continued liquids. Maintaining one's normal sleep and feed patterns during a trip helps. Time zone crossing is handled many ways. Some choose a flight that arrives at the hour which normally begins the workday or, alternatively, that arrives at the usual bedtime hour—so they may immediately go to sleep. Another option is to arrive for an important meeting two or more days early and prepare by relaxing. Finally, some prefer to reset their body clock several days before leaving home by developing a sleep-wake cycle similar to the clock hours at the destination.

Kure

There are many conventional aids for this widespread malady, and I can add a few to the pot after having crossed thousands of time zones. Arrive hours early at the airport and spend time kicking back. Distraction works so bring a cliffhanger book. The amenities of flying business or first class are effective if affordable.

Once after a month on a 13-country investigative tour for a speculator I felt myself becoming dull. I upgraded the tickets and used other Kures to get sharp in a couple of days. In my opinion, physical fitness is directly proportional to resistance to symptoms. Keep the body's internal works traveling with lots of liquid; take your own in quantity onto the plane. I also pack a first meal in case the flight, train, or bus is delayed. Some authorities advise eating less to beat traveler's malaise, but I disagree, eating more so long as liquids are available to wash it along. Finally, the "redeye" or night trip is a favorite because I sleep during transport and awake fresh as if never having moved.

I divide traveler's syndrome into two categories: short-term and long-term. The short-term version occurs in the first couple of days due to the stresses of haste, change in schedule, and crossing time zones. The long-term condition comes weeks or months into the trip and is due to being intense for too long. The former has been covered, and the latter is common among my round-the-world ticket traveling peers whose journeys extend up to a year. I've seen them raving or crying without knowing why and, similarly, I've weathered bouts a couple of times with an insight:

Force yourself every three weeks to stay in one place for a few days, preferably a white-sand island resort. During twenty years of nearly constant travel to a hundred countries, the longest swing was 18 months through Africa and South America. I learned that, with periodic rest breaks, chronic traveler's illness doesn't crop up.

Whether short or long term, spend the first day at a new spot taking it easy. Continue to eat and drink well, and add an hour of sleep that night. I wear nightshades and earplugs during plane, bus, or train trips to decrease sensory input. The best tip to health during travel is to pack a pair of running shoes. The first step upon new turf should be a sightseeing jog.

VISION PROBLEMS

What is it?

This entry is intentionally general. It includes far-sightedness, near-sightedness, lazy eye, photophobia, glaucoma, cataracts, double vision, detached retina, and more, especially from a neurological viewpoint.

Traditional Treatment

One customarily goes without forethought to an ophthalmologist (eye doctor) who prescribes aids.

Kure

Better vision can be had without glasses. Find books on your library shelf, if you like, on eye exercises for various conditions. I've tried their techniques and heartily recommend them for simple conditions like near- or far-sightedness and some others. I postulated the use of eye exercises to improve vision because of a background in anatomy before coming across the books. The eyeball is like a Ping-Pong ball attached by muscles all around to its bony orbit. The eye also accommodates for distance using lens muscles, and the iris is muscular. So seeing is much under voluntary control, akin to lifting weights in that one can strengthen and coordinate the muscles.

I am a substitute schoolteacher and one way to grab class attention is by holding a book upside down and reading aloud. "How?" is the reaction, and I reply, "This reminds me of the child who was handed a violin and asked if he could play. He said he didn't know because he hadn't tried yet." Then my class turns their books upside down and begins reading bottom-to-top, right-to-left easily. That is the lead-in to a course I once offered at a community college, "The art and science of backward reading and writing," and is also the best exercise Kure for general vision problems.

Note: *Most up-to-date computer operating systems enable you to invert the screen image (basically rotate the image on your screen 180 degrees) by pressing Ctrl-Alt-DownArrow, which enables you to read a text page from right to left and from bottom to top. [Return to the normal view by Ctrl-Alt-UpArrow.] Try spelling your eyes by such "reversing the flow" for a minute of every hour you deal with text on screen; you'll be amazed at the results.*

The backward reading idea began after I won some national paddleball titles and decided to switch to the opposite hand for competition. I was a natural righty with strong backhand that I secretly attributed to having longhand-written so much material. The motion of moving a pen across a paper from left to right is remarkably similar to the swing motion of any sport's backhand, so I began writing in mirror image with the left hand with the goal of a proficient backhand. Within a year I was placing well with both hands in tournaments and dreaming of meeting myself in the finals righty vs. lefty.

Convinced I was on to something with the backward (mirror) writing, I looked for ways to read in same, trying a mirror at first and then turning books by the dozens upside down. Later I would type pages by the thousands with the computer monitor upside down. I began to notice a visual difference too.

If you like to read and want greater strength and stamina, try this: Read an hour with the book positioned normally for 15 minutes, turn it upside down for the next 15 minutes and alternate throughout the hour. You'll have unbelievable stamina and eventually be able to read continually for hours. It's like curling a weight with one hand, then resting that muscle while you curl with the other. Do you do sports like baseball, tennis, soccer, boxing, or basketball? If so, try backward reading to cause your eyes to track objects better from right to left. Words in a sentence flow like sports balls, and when you practice reading with flow from right to left you automatically improve your athletic vision.

Next, go to go to mirror image writing. That's what I did after discovering the advantages of backward reading. Leonardo da Vinci called it his secret mirror code, but I developed it independently. At school I write an assignment on the board and the girls pull out their compact mirrors and read it aloud. I show the class how to practice writing the mirror alphabet and simple words, as I had done in learning.

Words in a sentence flow
like sports balls, and when
you practice reading with
flow from right to left you
automatically improve
your athletic vision.

We are a visual society, bombarded by the second with print that flows left to right. I hypothesize we are visual versions of hunchbacks, overdeveloped on one side. This causes eyestrain, headaches, neck and back strain (ref. "Neck Stiffness," page 59). Turn a book upside down and after reading a while find as others have that they suddenly adopt a different head, neck, and back posture and their little pains disappear. Many visual problems improve also. If convinced of this Kure, the next step is writing in mirror image and turning computer monitors upside down (press control-alt-⇩ as noted above).

Any monitor should be set at eye level or slightly higher. Placing the monitor higher than normal corrects a lot of neck and back strain since the head is like a bowling ball with muscle attachments at the neck to keep it from rolling off. With this more relaxed posture the eyes function better in the long haul (ref. "Neck Stiffness," page 59).

Some other tips: Dim the contrast. Pick a print that is sans-sans, i.e. simple and pleasing to the eye; I prefer Arial in 8-point. Use black-and-white rather than color. I've learned to see things around me and recall them in black and white because recall is quicker, more acute, and the after-image disappears more rapidly. It isn't as pretty or fun, but that's the trade-off. These applications hold for TVs too.

I was a child diagnosed as myopic, photophobic, strabismic (lazy eye), and having one of the worst cases of depth perception the doctor had ever seen. I conquered these without glasses or professional help, and encourage others to try the same Kures before consulting an expert. Note that the book you hold in your hands, *Keeley's Kures*, was born when I got an email from photojournalist friend Art Shay, who was having a terrible time with double-vision. "I've been to all the specialists and nothing works."

I introduced him to eye exercises, backward reading and writing, and made some changes in his computer habits. As his eyesight improved I got an email, "You ought to write a book." One day perhaps this book—or at least this chapter—will be printed in mirror image and sold with an attached mirror as a training aid. ☺

WARTS

What is it?

A benign, often persistent skin growth caused by a virus infection and found most commonly on the hands, soles of the feet, elbow or face. Appearance depends on location and type. They are only mildly contagious (except the genital variety) and not spread by direct contact. People with weakened immune systems are more susceptible. Toads have wart-like bumps but humans don't get warts from handling them.

Traditional Treatment

The usual technique is to wait for spontaneous disappearance within two years. Others include over-the-counter wart-removal medications (usually containing salicylic acid), freezing them off with liquid nitrogen, destruction with caustic chemicals, laser surgery, and electrocautery (burning them off with an electric current).

Kure

The list of treatments is impressive and my contribution is to arrange them into an itinerary.

Rule of Thumb

Begin any disease treatment with the most conservative therapy and advance to the most aggressive or expensive.

Start with a removal medication and experiment one-at-a-time until reaching treatments that require a doctor. Don't scratch or itch at the bump, and stay in shape to keep the immune system roaring. The most annoying wart is situated where it receives irritation, so if it's under the fingernails or on the sole of the feet you may choose the more aggressive therapy.

For face warts use an electric razor or grow a beard to cut down on nicks which create virus entry points. Consider preparations from your herbal pharmacy such as dandelion latex or birch bark.

Like other people, I've had and conquered warts down to the proverbial last one: Hanging on for so many years that I began to admire it, one still sat atop my right index finger knuckle where it caught edges that reinvited the virus. It carried me around for ten years defying every treatment and wish, until I went to India.

I've had and conquered warts down to the last one, including the little rascal on my finger hanging on for so many years I began to admire it.

A thin guide led me down a cobblestone street jammed with shanties in a Bombay shipyard to a closed blue door. "This is 'the doctor,'" he hollered, and the door magically opened. A teenager in soiled rags slipped out clutching an antique leather medical case. He cracked it with a squeak to reveal a neat arrangement of scalpels, suction cups, hoses and medicine vials. He turned all attention to the knuckle in a gathering circle of shipyard ragamuffins and inquisitive neighbors; kids crawled out windows, and a cow peeked out a front door. He was so professional and the case so worn that I forgot his youth and dirty rags.

"This is what wart roots look like," 'the doctor' announced, shaking a vial of gray slivers that resembled half-inch flukes. The crowd gasped, and so I resisted asserting that everyone in the West knows warts have no roots. Nor did I argue as he set the fee at a buck a root.

He snatched a scalpel, demonstrated its keen edge on a dirty shirt, and took my finger in a steady hand. He lopped off the wart onto the street without ceremony or anesthesia. Spurting blood threw the circle of watchers back, but only for a moment. "Now for the roots!" he drew them in. A quick hand movement produced a suction thimble that fell atop the red wound. In-and-out it squeezed the liquid up… then, 'the doctor' held high the cup.

"Roots!" he shouted, and poured a thimbleful of blood and gook onto a cobblestone. "Count them: One, two, three, four… and five!" They wiggled like tiny worms in soup.

The scamp extended his other hand, as I haggled the fee down to $3, which he quickly swiped.

"Jungle powder!" he declared, and sprinkled black powder from a vial onto the wound, pressing it in with his forefinger. "Go in peace," he said, lifting it. "The wart is gone."

The crowd left, the cow pulled in its head, 'The doctor' closed his case, and the wart never returned.

How To Treat Anything for Starters

For starters, your physician should be a sports medicine doctor, or at least an elderly physician. It makes all the difference in treatment and recovery. A lot may also be said for a specialist or clinic dealing only in a specific ailment, since they base treatments on personal conclusions from having seen thousands of cases. Get a second opinion, if possible, definitely seek recovered peers for advice, and search online for the key words: disease name, forum, and natural treatments.

Health Insurance

What is the one thing everyone needs but cannot afford, hence the single string to control a person, families, and whole societies' lives? Health insurance. If overpriced, it cuts out the middle class—the rich can afford it, the middle class teeters in ill health, and the poor get it free with enough time to wait in hospital lines and pick up bugs.

The ramifications of unaffordable insurance are sundry. One frets about getting ill, and so becomes. Aspiring youth are forced out of entrepreneurship into government, military, and corporate jobs *with benefits*. I saw it daily while teaching school—the inability to go to the hospital for a skateboard crash, and the students geared study away from books to cultivating relationships to get jobs *with benefits*.

My SED (severely emotionally disturbed) class had many cases of the brightest kids and parents who invested their children in the class to get instant, free health insurance, and to build a future family breadwinner in the welfare system. Further, is it stupid to earn less salary to fall into a low-income bracket for free health care, as many do?

Long ago, I quit contributing to escalating monthly insurance premiums, and used cheap, comprehensive traveler's insurance while globetrotting. Now I travel without standard health insurance exclusively in third-world countries where medical/dental/hospital fees are about 1/50th that of the USA.

For example, I get a physical and medical workup on arriving and leaving South America for $50; a tooth crown ground and repegged on the spot in México for $5; and local healer/shaman doctors from Indonesia to the Amazon treat everything from blisters to stomach aches for a song. One can hardly live in America without health insurance, yet who can afford it? I like to say, don't point out a fault without a solution. I don't have an answer for American health insurance, except to make it accessible even if it means the one thing to socialize, but learn self-treatment (e.g. the Kures) at the same time.

Medical Tourism

This is valuable info for an ex-pat or American in need of competent medical care. A traveler or US resident willing to take a junket to a five-star hotel + quality hospital in an exotic land need not have American medical insurance, considering the low rates Third World countries charge for diagnosis, treatment, and operations. (Someone pointed out to me that it is correctly termed medical rather than health insurance, because many overwrought American doctors are ill at promoting your health.)

It's all in finding the right doctor, anywhere. I insist on older docs and sports med physicians, or at least one who does sports. In a dearth, visit a sharp young clinic operation of a handful of friendly docs who in synergy come up with the proper diagnosis and treatment. My luck with physicians in foreign countries has been excellent. They kick up the 'homey' price 20% for ex-pats or visitors, bringing it to maybe 5% of American rates.

Foreign hospital doctors nearly always have private practices at home, and that's where I get instant professional help. No appointment, his wife is the secretary, and he's linked to the top specialists for radiology, lab tests, surgery, and so on in town. You're in and out the door in 15 minutes, and feeling so much better for it that you're tempted to not even fill the prescription down the block instantly at about 25% USA costs. The doctors and pharmacists generally speak some English.

Foreign docs, while making less than American, often own businesses on the side. I got close to an Iquitos, Peru, waitress to meet the physician-owner of a restaurant who gave me a tour of his clinic, some excellent off-the-cuff health pointers, and was willing to trade English lessons for future diagnoses.

On the other hand, here in Lake Toba, Sumatra, the elderly lady who just made me a salad says that no one in Toba gets sick, and there are no dentists (she's never been), but for a village accident or emergency you are whisked away in one of three cars to a nearby town where the doctor accepts homemade pies and chickens, just as the old-time American doctors.

> *... for a village accident or emergency one is whisked away in one of three cars to a nearby town where the doctor accepts homemade pies and chickens, just as the old-time American doctors.*

Medical tourism is a welcome wave set off by American shock-fees. However, after the Bumrungrad, Bangkok, hospital was ruined following a TV special five years ago—medical tourism, caused by the TV show, increased so rapidly that its health care grew shoddy and foreigners retreated—foreign providers have learned it's all about the competition.

Likewise, it's reckoned that USA prices will fall with less demand. Or, they'll try to control it somehow, like recently 'requiring' American passports to reenter from Mexico, where thousands of borderline Americans travel for medical and dental Rxs. The truth at the border—tested by friends and me dozens of times and most recently six months ago—is when a smart-alec immigration officer demands your passport or else, the results-oriented legal repartee is that he may not prevent you from entering your own country. Then his face reddens, and he waves a sheet in your face that asks you next time to bring a passport.

Cancer and AIDS

Only in a pinch would I get chemo or radiation treatments for cancer. They're over-prescribed as the concurred treatments among traditional doctors to avoid lawsuits. The results, in more than half the cases, are worse than the original condition.

Many people, perhaps a majority of seniors, trot around healthily with undiagnosed cancer, and pass on just short of 100 years. The tragedy, repeated a million times over, is the old guy goes in for a checkup, a questionable, nonsymptomatic growth is unearthed (that probably would remain so for life), a biopsy done, CANCER screamed, and the slow chemo or radiation death 'cure' starts. (Ref. below.)

The Delicate Address of AIDS

In the mid-1990s, I spent a few weeks globetrotting to Canada, Europe, and the alternative medicine Livingston-Wheeler Clinic in San Diego to gather information on Acquired Immunodeficiency Syndrome (AIDS) and cancer for a concerned group. Since witnessing and touching my first pancreatic cancer in 1968 (in a young male boxer) as a wet-behind-the-ears veterinarian—and glamorization of what I believe is, for the most part, a scheme by the AMA to fleece the American public while covering its royal buttocks—I arrived at an unpopular conclusion that cancer's primary cause is a compromised host.

I arrived at an unpopular conclusion that cancer's primary cause is a compromised host.

This is an unfit person or unhealthy organ, usually from diet or environment that enables a secondary agent (virus) to step in to rev up compromised cell metabolism and *party*—with replication and leaving a mess just like a frat scene. Microbes are everywhere, despite ammonia and handy wipes. In fact, because of popular disinfectants microbes have evolved wisely not to kill the host or organs too quickly, or else the party won't linger.

So, what's to be done about cancer?

The present treatments of radiation and chemotherapy are slipshod, often killing a patient before his time. I believe a majority of cancer patients are better off never finding out and living a full, healthy, symptomless life. Of American seniors, I personally believe 80% of the tiny spots of cancer go unnoticed with *zero* bearing on health and life quality, until RIP. Cancer isn't the monster it's shouted to be.

If a cure is found, the odds are it will be an injection directly into the cancerous tissue, rather than a systemic treatment that debilitates (further compromises) the health of the patient. Remember that doctors are called upon to "do something," even if it's worse than nothing. They must follow conventional guidelines and drum up business for the Pharmaceutical Machine, or get sued for malpractice. This is one reason to take a medical tourism junket to an exotic country for an annual checkup.

Likely, the direct injection into a cancer will come from the Amazon green pharmacy—the most fecund evolutionary brew the earth has known. I've gone collecting there *with*, been treated *by*, and know that western medicine may profit *from* jungle shamans (healers). They treat holistically, sizing up a patient's lifestyle, before prescribing jungle medicines, chants, and/or flower baths.

The Belen witches of Iquitos, Peru, operate along a bright alley on a waterfront market, a dozen standing before 10-foot-tall shelves of bottles of custom herbs and tonics for prescription. The 'patient,' often a First-World traveler, approaches the healer of choice who appraises him with a penetrating glance for skin tone, eye brightness, lip gloss, hair health, posture, and other things I don't know about. Sometimes they take a pulse; however, from vet med where animals are speechless, as in foreign tongues, there is no need for dialog.

The last fresh therapy is that American doctors would serve better medicines for cancer and other ailments by dining at a Thai restaurant… and ducking into the kitchen to discover why it tastes so good. Thai chefs are the most adept in the world at mixing ingredients to affect the tongue, intestinal tract, blood organs, and then nervous tissue. Their dishes are a medley of time-release ingredients that act in concert. Eating Thai is a synergy.

The last fresh therapy is that American doctors would serve better medicines for cancer and other ailments by dining at a Thai restaurant.

Medicines should be prepared in the same harmonious blends. This targets localized cancer to attack in gentle waves, so as not to shock the surrounding tissues and general health. And, a lesson from vet school is that temperature makes a difference. The rate of absorption of oral (tablet or liquid) medicines along the intestinal tract is controlled by temperature, and drinking one glass of tepid water with each dilutes and washes the medicines along.

Cancer may be beaten, or at least the tide turned, by recognizing the primary cause as a compromised host or tissue, a holistic approach, medicines from the green pharmacy, a Thai-like blend, and a rigorous American scientific approach to discover a cure, unhampered by pharmaceutic leagues.

AIDS was also part of my world search for a 1990s sponsor, and continues today. From this, I offer a couple of grody insights into the condition that I think, like cancer, is 90% American Hoax. Yet, it exists, so let's be direct.

A veterinarian's periodic chore, especially for poodles and Pomeranians, is to express (relieve of contents) the anal gland. After a few of these, it becomes easy to talk about. Plus, I got an image from homosexual Amazon hairdressers (who monopolize the business) of the 'corazon' (Spanish for heart). Confirmed by the standard source, *Gray's Anatomy*, just inside the anus lies a throbbing venous ring the hairdressers call the 'corazon' ('little darling'). Bluntly, during anal sex, this ring may be abraded, and bleed like hemorrhoids.

No one with a bruised or torn 'heart,' or risky hemorrhoids, should engage in anal sex, and I don't care what everyone else does. (One shocked friend in my informal email practice wrote after my Rx to stop it, "You sure know a lot about a_holes!") The reason to stop is that all that's in there, unlike the female vagina, pounds into the venous abrasion… and directly into the blood stream. Infected bisexual males may mate with females to pass it on.

This politically ignored logic is probably the primary cause of AIDS' symptoms, or at least it compromises the immune system to allow a secondary cause everyone is searching for. The Amazon hairdressers, with business in a downswing, may become the site of a controlled experiment to take the mystery out of AIDS.

When decades of convention pass, repeated to little success, this is a definition of insanity and it's time to strike out for new ideas on AIDS… and cancer.

Bugs

A different perspective on microbes:

Being a universal host of diseases doesn't win close friends, but keeps one busy. At an early age, I started admiring microbes, including pathogens, under a progression of more powerful microscopes, and falling in love: Who could resist the fuzzy *paramecium*, whiptail *euglena*, and amorphous *amoeba* that nonetheless would try to bring me to my knees? What linguist hears without a heart flutter *spherophorus necrophorus*, *entamoeba histolytica*, and *caseous adenosis*?

So, one by one, I contracted them. By 1994, I paged through the *Merck Medical Manual* physician's bible (that as a veterinary intern I dashed to the plumber's closet to pillage the vet version to diagnose waiting pets on the examination tables). What I found was that I'd encountered and recovered from about 35% of the vast listings of ailments known to mankind, including the obscure Hobo Disease.

A decade later, I bragged to my physician to relieve his anxiety over my first renal calculi, and he starred in stony silence. He then quoted Abraham Lincoln at the Wisconsin Agricultural Fair, "This too shall pass...."

Since visiting the Amazon and South Pacific and adding bouts of malaria, elephantiasis, and hepatitis, my exposure rate tops 50% or 65%—including the ridiculous psychiatric section.

Each microbe, from childhood, is a study, and produces two where there was one in a blink, for pain or for pleasure. The reason for the lifelong loves is that a recovered peer is the best medical help you can find anywhere. So if you become afflicted and run into me out there in the wilderness, or in the teeming cities of the world, rest assured I'll have made a continuing running head start on my Hippocratic Oath.

On Vets and Meds

If I seem out of place in strange diagnoses with odd treatments of human ailments, it's only because people aren't accustomed to a veterinarian addressing human medicine. Vets, many smarter than I, take the same courses as human medicine students but have a long edge in seeing more patients. How many more? About 30 times.

We walk lines of kennels and circle pastures while a physician is limited to his practice and hospitals. Vets take a holistic approach to treatment that should be applied to human medicine, accounting for the weather to what kind of scraps Farmer John's wife throws to the pigs. We diagnose by gaze and touch more than by dialog and lab tests.

Vets are not specialists, and have been trained in the anatomy, diagnosis, and treatment of four species: dog, cat, cow and horse. Finally, the two vets I worked for treated their own kids, from stitches to prescriptions, in their clinic. Masterful human physicians abound, but if I had kids who got sick, I would tell them to first go to a veterinarian and get a second opinion from a physician.

ABOUT THE AUTHOR[2]

Steven 'Bo' Keeley is a Doctor of Veterinary Medicine, former national racquet champion, and has traveled the world… on a wing and a shoestring.

"My life has followed the vicissitudes of Buck the Dog in Jack London's *Call of the Wild*: from comfortable back yards across America; boxcars on every major railroad; 100+ countries under a backpack; hiking the lengths of Florida, Colorado, Vermont, California, Death Valley, and Baja; to retirement in a desert burrow with Sir the Rattlesnake as a doorkeep… and a solar computer to write essays and memoirs."

In 2007, he became the first California substitute teacher—most requested by students and faculty—to be fired surrounding a 'playground war.' He left to ride the rails, and then became an itinerant expatriate writing from selective global Shangri-Las including Iquitos, Peru, San Felipe, Baja, and, lately, unspoiled Lake Toba, Sumatra.

Bo's Wikipedia entry reads like Indiana Jones.

---

[2] "The picture is at 14,000 ft. in the Peruvian Andes where a dog with the red-eye condition, and 10-year old girl waltzed in front of me on an empty street. They danced, she leading, he on hind legs, with a red moon hanging on the wall behind me. So I sat, traded the camera for the dog... a magic moment, and then cover material for Keeley's Kures."

INDEX

A

B

C

D

E

F

G

H

L

M

N

O

P

Q

R

S

T

U

V

W

Made in the USA
Charleston, SC
24 April 2011